C000115792

The Complete Keto Diet for Two #2019

<u>5-Ingredient Affordable, Quick & Simple Ketogenic Recipes | Lose Weight, Balance Hormones, Boost Brain Health, and Reverse Disease | 21-Day Keto Meal Plan</u>

Dr Zachare Jasoner

© Copyright 2019 Dr Zachare Jasoner - All Rights Reserved.

In no way is it legal to reproduce, duplicate, or transmit any part of this document by either electronic means or in printed format. Recording of this publication is strictly prohibited, and any storage of this material is not allowed unless with written permission from the publisher. All rights reserved.

The information provided herein is stated to be truthful and consistent, in that any liability, regarding inattention or otherwise, by any usage or abuse of any policies, processes, or directions contained within is the solitary and complete responsibility of the recipient reader. Under no circumstances will any legal liability or blame be held against the publisher for any reparation, damages, or monetary loss due to the information herein, either directly or indirectly.
Respective authors own all copyrights not held by the publisher.

Legal Notice:

This book is copyright protected. This is only for personal use. You cannot amend, distribute, sell, use, quote or paraphrase any part of the content within this book without the consent of the author or copyright owner. Legal action will be pursued if this is breached.

Disclaimer Notice:

Please note the information contained within this document is for educational and entertainment purposes only. Every attempt has been made to provide accurate, up-to-date and reliable, complete information. No warranties of any kind are expressed or implied. Readers acknowledge that the author is not engaging in the rendering of legal, financial, medical or professional advice.

By reading this document, the reader agrees that under no circumstances are we responsible for any losses, direct or indirect, which are incurred as a result of the use of information contained within this document, including, but not limited to, errors, omissions, or inaccuracies.

Table of contents

Introduction

Several dietary approaches today exist in the world. Every diet promises a different taste and a set of new health benefits. In today's ever-challenging lifestyle, we all need a single formula plan to get all the health benefits at a time. In this context, the Ketogenic diet plan offers a tempting solution. The diet has been in use for several decades. Research and extensive studies in this field has allowed the food experts to create a diet that could provide solution to all the health problems whether its obesity, cardiac diseases, diabetes, cholesterol etc. For every family structure such a diet finds a great important. This cookbook is therefore written to provide all the secrets of ketogenic diet. After a precise and accurate account of the ketogenic diet, the book discloses number of tempting recipes to suit everyone's daily needs including desserts, breakfasts, exotic entrees and homely meals.

Chapter 1: Why Cook for Two

The basic family structure has evolved everywhere in the world. The traditional units have collapsed to raise a new nuclear structure. The concept of family has changed many folds over the years; today, two friends or loved ones also make up a family together. We, therefore, need more recipes and meals which could meet the needs of such family structures. Now everyone earns for himself and cooks for himself. In such a society, cooking a meal with a large number of servings is futile or useless and a waste of resource. In this cookbook, we shall be discussing the recipes which can serve two individuals easily. Whether a person is a student living far away from home or living with a friend or a partner, these recipes can suit his or her needs perfectly.

Chapter 2: The Basics of Keto Diet

What is Keto Diet

When we think of any particular Low Carb dietary plan, the word ketogenic instantly pops up in our minds. That is mainly because the Ketogenic diet is highly effective in its results. Many people find the ketogenic diet highly restrictive too, but that again helps in achieving better health goals. The diet originated as a result of experimental studies to treat patients of Parkinson or epilepsy through dietary changes. Researchers found out that having high fat and low carbohydrates in the diet can result in positive change in the mental and physical health of the patients. Those who opted this diet started to improve on their mental condition and other health symptoms were also observed in them. From there on Ketogenic diet started to take its present shape. All food items containing a high amount of carbohydrates were marked forbidden in the diet. Moreover, the focus was shifted towards fat as a source of energy. It was discovered that maintaining a low level of carbohydrates in the daily diet, and high amount of fat can force the body to metabolize using fat only, which releases three times more energy and releases ketones during their digestion.

In a ketogenic diet, every meal should not contain more than 10-15 grams of carbohydrates in them. Since carbohydrates are easy to breakdown, the human body instantly digest them to release quick energy, fats are only processed in the absence of carbohydrates, this can only be made possible by reducing the carb intake to extremely low levels as prescribed by the ketogenic diet. All fruits, vegetables, sugars, sweeteners, grains, etc., containing a high amount of carbohydrates are completely restricted on this diet, whereas fat and protein-rich meat, vegetables, dairy products, etc. are completely allowed.

How Keto is different from other diets

A ketogenic diet is distinctive from all the other health-oriented diets for several reasons. Firstly, it fully restricts the consumption of carbohydrates in the diet. It points out carbs as enemies of good health and active metabolism. Not only it restricts the intake but also set a standard formula to limit the number of carbohydrates taken per meal. The diet is not only restrictive in essence, but also suggestive. It promotes the use of good quality fats in food products. If it restricts carbs for one reason, it provides a rather healthy alternative.

The ketogenic diet works progressively to reveal its results and effects on human health. It does not restrict the overall consumption of food and its amount per meal, but it focuses on the prohibition of certain macronutrients like carbohydrates. It guarantees not only physical fitness but also an improved mental condition. Ketogenic diet prescribes several alternatives to high carb food. Due to excess research in this field and increased demand, the food industry has been able to produce keto friendly products.

How does the Ketogenic diet works?

The principle behind the success of the ketogenic diet is twofold; firstly, it prohibits the intake of carbohydrates then promotes the increased consumption of fats. A high-fat food in the absence of excess carb initiates the process of ketosis in the human body. Ketosis is the breakdown of fat molecules to release energy and other products, including ketones. A fat molecule contains strong bonds in its triglycerides. Every time a single fat molecule breaks down, it releases three times greater energy than the breakdown of a single carbohydrate molecule. Carbohydrates are known for providing instant energy to the body as they are easier and quicker to digest. That is why every time we feel weak and goes through hypoglycemia; we look for something sweet and carb-rich to consume immediately. Since not all the carbs cannot be consumed by the body at once, all the excess carbs along with the dietary fats we take in, are stored in the body, eventually causing obesity, heart diseases, diabetes-insulin resistance, and low metabolic rates.

On the other hand, if fats are consumed instead as the mere source of energy, they take time to digest and releases energy gradually and progressively. Along with energy fats are capable of producing ketones, these are antioxidant agents which can fight against harmful radicals and toxins in the body. It is due to these ketones that the ketogenic diet works best for mental reverberations. The ketones clean up all the toxic waste that results from brain activity. Ketosis is the driving force that makes the ketogenic diet work. It can be achieved by maintaining the per meal carb intake up to 13 grams and increasing the amount of fat.

Ketosis has several other known benefits, which indirectly improves human health. The production of ketones increases the production of mitochondria in the cells. The mitochondria are the powerhouse of the cells; their increased production cause a boost in energy. The production is particularly increased in the brain cells. This increased energy indirectly accelerates the rate of metabolism in the body. Mitochondrial production can sustain the better health of the cells.

The aging nerve cells can be repaired with the high production of ketones in the body. Ketones help in the reproduction of the damaged nerve cells and support in case of the nervous system malfunction. Many research studies have suggested that ketones can help to treat brain damage and injuries. Ketones are more effective fuel than ordinary sugar. Ketosis is responsible for producing a lesser number of free radicals and oxidants than the complete digestion of carbohydrates. By used ketones as the fuel, overall damage to the body is reduced as it removed those free radicals and oxidants.

Several types of researches have been conducted on the impact of ketosis over the development of cancer. Ketones producing as a result of ketosis also help in containing the development of cancer cells. When the ketones are processed, the resulting energy cannot be consumed by the cancer cells for their growth. When these cells cease to gain energy, they are easily eliminated by the natural immune system of the body.

When it comes to brain functioning, ketones have the most evident effects. All the early researches had progressively worked on the relation between ketones and mental health. The studies have revealed that people suffering from Parkinson's, Alzheimer, autism, and epilepsy, when put on a ketogenic diet showed improved condition. Such brain conditions cannot be fully treated Ketones have an inhibitory effect on brain cells. When hyper excited brain cells cause seizures and autism-like behavior, those ketones prevent their hyperactivity and lessen such symptoms of brain malfunctioning.

There are several other benefits of ketosis, which are proven through rigorous research. Besides "ketoacidosis" and Keto flu, there are no marked negative effects of ketogenic diet and ketosis.

How to know when you are in Ketosis?

This is perhaps the most commonly asked question every beginner puts out there while opting the ketogenic diet. There is no fixed one formula to determine whether the body has undergone ketosis. For some people a week of the complete ketogenic diet is enough to create a shift, for some, this may take days or for others might few weeks. It all depends upon the individual body chemistry, the metabolic rates, existing lifestyle, dietary changes, and daily routine. Ketones strips test is commonly recommended, but that again only indicates the level of ketones the body is excreting, not the level of ketosis occurring inside.

There is yet another method commonly prescribed that is to check blood glucose using a monitor, but it is too expensive and does not rightly indicates the occurring of the ketosis. However, there are few visible signs and symptoms which can rightly indicate that a body is going through ketosis. Again, the timings of the visibility of these signs vary for each individual. Here is the list of those symptoms:

1. Excessive Urination

Ketones are known as a natural diuretic, which means that they aid in the removal of the extra water out of the body through urination. So high ketone levels mean increased urination than normal. Due to ketosis, Acetoacetate is released three times faster than the usual, which is also excreted along with urine, which in turn cause more urination.

2. Dry Mouth

It is obvious that increased urination causes dehydration as more fluids are released out of the body due to ketosis. Along with fluids, many important electrolytes and metabolites are also expelled out of the body. Therefore, it is recommended to increase the consumption of water and electrolytes to maintain the water table of the body while a person is on the ketogenic diet. Having salty things like pickles etc. in the routine meal can also help in maintaining water levels in the body.

3. Bad Breath

A ketone named acetone is released partially through our breast. This ketone does not have a good smell, and it takes longer time to disappear. Due to ketosis, a good number of acetones is released in the breath, causing bad breath. It can be controlled by using a good mouth fresh.

4. Reduced Hunger and Increased Energy

It is the most obvious sign of the ketosis. Since fat is a high energy macronutrient, and it takes longer duration indigestion, a person on high fat and low carb diet feel reduced appetite but a boost in the energy levels.

After witnessing all these signs together, there is no need left to check the ketone levels or check ketosis by monitoring your sugar levels. It is said that when an individual undergoes ketosis, he can feel the changes happening inside of him if all the signs discussed above are visible at a time.

The health benefits of Keto diet

The ketogenic diet is known for a variety of its health benefits. People with mental ailments use it for their brain cells repair; heart patients use it to get rid of bad cholesterol, diabetics use it to control their sugar levels and reduce insulin resistance where obese individuals use it to reduce their weight and trim down their body shape. Even the cancer patients are recommended to opt for a ketogenic diet for good health effects. How come a single diet can yield such multifaceted results? Let find out the varying degree of health benefits promised by the ketogenic diet.

1. Weight Loss

Reduction in body weight is the natural outcome of a diet low in carbohydrates and high in fat. Fat is usually considered the reason for obesity, but that is not true when we take such fat in the absence of carbs, they help in removing the accumulated fat in the body through active metabolism. As the sugar levels in the blood drops as a result of ketosis, the fat cell in different parts of the body travels to the liver and are processed to released ketones and energy. Due to the ketogenic diet, our body becomes a fat burning machine.

2. Control Blood Sugar

Naturally, the blood glucose levels are maintained with the help of hormones released by our pancreases- insulin and glucagon. People suffering from diabetes cannot produce insulin to counter the release of glucose in the blood. Consequently, it results in a high blood glucose level. Since the ketogenic diet does not contain any direct sugar or excess of carbohydrates, the glucose levels are maintained even in the absence of insulin. The insulin resistance in type II diabetic patients is also controlled by the ketogenic diet. the consistent and controlled blood sugar levels keep the diabetic patient healthy and active.

3. Mental Focus

Mental focus and improvement in brain functioning are the primary results of the ketogenic diet. The ketones it provides, repair the damaged brain cells, and activates a better nerve connection. Carbs release harmful toxins and oxidants, which pollutes the brain' internal environment. Whereas the ketones act as anti-oxidants and allow cleaning of this toxic build up. Moreover, brain cells are composed largely of fatty acids, and only a fat-rich diet can nourish them well. High dose of fatty acids can boost the mental functions up to many folds. s

4. Increase in Energy

Boost in the energy levels is the result of the increased mitochondrial production. As already discussed here, the ketones are responsible for supporting mitochondrial generation, which accelerates the release of energy. Moreover, ketones are a more reliable source of energy than glucose as its level can alleviate the decrease in carb intake. A ketogenic diet also supports an active metabolism which adds up to the overall energy production in the body.

5. Better Appetite Control

A carb-rich diet makes your hungrier every now and then. As carbs are an instant source, they are processed quickly to produce energy and leave a hungry body behind. Since fat takes a longer duration to digest, a ketogenic meal does not make a person hungry after a short period of time.

6. Epilepsy

Since the 1900s, the ketogenic diet has been strongly associated with the treatment of epilepsy. It is even used today to treat uncontrollable epilepsy in young children. It allows the patients to live a prolong and healthy lives without taking excessive medicines. Unlike medicinal therapies, the ketogenic diet has no serious side effects on both the mind and the body.

7. Cholesterol & Blood Pressure

The low-density lipoproteins LDL, also known as the bad cholesterol are responsible for several cardiovascular diseases as these fats can accumulate in the blood vessels and create an obstruction in the blood flow. On the other hand, High-density lipoproteins, HDL or good cholesterol, does not accumulate in the blood, rather it binds with LDL molecules along with it and excretes out of the body. A high-fat diet can guarantee these HDL molecules, which reduces the overall blood cholesterol levels and consequently, the blood pressure of the patients. Due to ketosis, all the excess fat molecules are broken down by the body to meet its energy needs.

8. Insulin Resistance

People suffering from type II diabetes do produce insulin in their bodies, but they somehow developed a resistance to insulin. As a result, the same hormone fails to accomplish its job. With the ketogenic diet, the sugar levels are already maintained due to fewer carbs in the meal. As a result; the insulin resistance can not cause much harm to the body.

9. Acne

A good diet directly reflects its good effects through the skin; Same is true for the Ketogenic diet, the anti-oxidants, released from the ketogenic meal can remove all the toxins from the skin cells and repair the already damaged cells. As a result, the skin starts to look fresh, smooth, radiation, and acne free.

8 Helpful Tips for Keto Journey

Every newbie can find his or her ketogenic journey difficult to continue. Abandoning all the carbs and switching to fat and proteins only is not a simple job, it requires a great deal of motivation plus constant efforts along with learning. In this world full of processed food products with a range of high carb meals, we need to be extra careful while opting for the ketogenic diet. Let's find out how we can make this journey easy on us without putting our mind and body through stress and hard labor.

1. Give up three meals a day

During the initial phase of the keto friendly diet, many people lose their appetite. This is quite normal, and loss appetite is not a concerning as long you are meeting all your caloric needs. The idea of three meals a day should be kept aside when it comes to the ketogenic diet. A good and complete is enough if taken twice in a week. You do not need to stress over three traditional meals in a day. Once your appetite goes back to normal, you can freely enjoy the third meal of the day. To keep your appetite normal, try exhausting yourself in routine exercises, cycling, swimming, jogging all can help.

2. A drizzle of vegetable oil

Whenever people are periled to take more fat, they start consuming all without any planning or scrutiny. Not fats are equally healthy; we all know that. Saturated fats should only be taken rarely, whereas unsaturated fats should make a good part of our ketogenic meal. To increase the fat content of your meal, try adding a drizzle of avocado or olive oil to every other meal. This drizzle can even give your food a good taste and loss of energy.

3. Reduce your protein intake to half

A low carb diet is mistakenly presumed to a high protein one which is completely wrong. If you are not consuming carbohydrates as per the usual intake, it does not mean that overconsuming proteins will meet the bodily needs and will boost the ketosis. It is quite the opposite; over-consumption of protein cannot do any good to the ketosis. Monicelli instead recommends reducing the protein consumption up to half. If a person takes eight pounds of steak in his normal diet then in a ketogenic diet, he should reduce the amount to four ounces on average.

4. Listen to your body

Our body is highly expressive of its needs. Don't be shy about embracing your new dietary routine. You can only incorporate the desired changes if you listen closely to your bodily needs. whether you can instantly switch to the ketogenic diet or you can adapt it gradually can only be assessed by analyzing the body condition, its sufferings, and rate of metabolism. What I usually recommend to newbies that they need to make gradual changes to their diet. Start by first cutting down direct sugars and fruits then switch replacing other ingredients full of carbs. After switching to a ketogenic diet, constantly check your blood sugar, cholesterol, and electrolyte levels. Consult your doctor or nutritionist if there is something serious.

5. Enjoy Variety

One of the major reasons people run away from the health-oriented diet plan is that they find them too boring and overly restrictive. Sure, the ketogenic diet is also a restrictive one, but you can make this diet all fun and interesting for you by adding the ingredients of your liking. Add more fruits and fresh vegetables. Enjoy the natural organic ingredients and try to explore all the different taste and varieties of ketogenic substitutes. Allow your taste buds to lead you to the right kind of meal. add more sauce, and side dishes to your ketogenic meal to make it more interesting and appealing.

6. Check the carbs in your favorite veggies

Make your eye a carb detector. Everything you eat should pass the scan of this detector. There are several vegetables, even a few of the green ones which are full of carb and should be avoided altogether. There are macronutrient calculators which can predict the number of carbs within each vegetable against the amount taken. Use such tools and create the habit of reading into labels of the food products, even the sauces, and condiment to control your carb intake.

7. Do what's best for your health

Just because everyone is opting the diet for its obvious effects, does not mean you should too blindly follow this dietary approach. If you are not comfortable with the plan or feeling sick or weak, then maybe you are doing it wrong, or your body is not ready for it. Before forcing anything on yourself, try consulting a professional who can rightly guide towards the major issues whether it's your body or the food you are taking, is causing the problem.

8. Know the risks

If you are aware of all the pros of a ketogenic diet, you must also be aware of the risks involved so that you could better prepare yourself. For pregnant ladies, ketogenic is not a suitable diet. If they are already consuming the ketogenic diet, then probably they should consult a health expert after conceiving the child. Extremely high levels of ketones are also life-threatening in extreme cases like that of Ketoacidosis. It can occur in patients of diabetes Miletus. Therefore, diabetic patients should be extra careful before switching to this low carb diet plan.

Chapter 3: Foods to Eat

The ketogenic dietary approach draws a distinct line for all of its followers. The line separates the high carb ingredients from the low carb ones. There is no in between, for a meal to be containing less than 15 grams of carbohydrates it must content minimum carb containing ingredients. Other than such those, all the food items are allowed to consume in your diet. Here is a raw list of the food products which can be used on a keto diet. All other processed products containing these ingredients are also safe to use.

- Meat Items

There is no restriction on protein intake; therefore, meat in any form is completely allowed on a ketogenic diet. Meat contains only proteins and fats, so they make a good part of a ketogenic diet. Whether it's the seafood, poultry: chicken, turkey, duck; beef, mutton, lamb, pork, etc. every meat is allowed on a diet.

- Keto Friendly Vegetables

All low carb vegetables are keto friendly. Unfortunately, there is not a single yardstick to categories such as vegetables. We can look for the number of the carb's vegetables have. Generally, all the vegetables grown above the ground contain lesser carbohydrates like vegetable greens, leeks, asparagus, chilies, lemon, etc. Other than this onion, tomatoes, ginger, garlic, zucchini, etc are also keto friendly vegetables.

- Seeds and Nuts

Seeds and dry nuts do not contain a high dose of carbohydrates, and a balanced intake of these nuts and seeds can be taken on a keto diet including the Pumpkin seeds, pistachio, almonds, walnuts, pecans, etc.

- Dairy Items

Most of the dairy products are keto friendly except the "Milk," since milk is a raw item it contains high traces of carbohydrates. However, when the milk is processed to get cheese, cream, cream cheese and yogurt, etc, the carbohydrates are broken down into other by-products. Therefore, all these products are allowed on the ketogenic diet. Instead of milk, we can use the following plant-based milk substitutes.

1. Soy milk
2. Hemp milk
3. Almond milk

4. Coconut milk
5. Macadamia milk

Ghee, butter, and eggs can also be enjoyed on a ketogenic diet plan.

- Ketogenic Fruits

There are several fruits which are full of sugars, and they can't be taken on this diet. Other than those the low carb fruits like blueberries, avocado, strawberries, raspberries, blackberries, coconut, cranberries, etc are all allowed on the ketogenic diet.

- All Fats

There is no restriction on the consumption of the fat. Therefore, any plant-based oil and animal-based ghee is completely allowed on this diet. Some of the commonly used cooking oil include olive oil, avocado oil, sesame oil, and canola oil.

- Keto-Sweeteners

Fear of cutting down the sweetness from their meals is what hit every ketogenic dieter the most. But the diet only restricts the carb intake not stops you from adding sweetness by using other substitutes. There are several keto friendly sweeteners available in the market today, including the following.

1. Erythritol
2. Monk fruit sweetener
3. Stevia
4. Swerve
5. Natvia

It is crucial to know that the intensity of sweetness and taste vary in each of those sweeteners. Not all of them can exactly replace with the same amount of sugars. Stevia is two hundred times sweeter than sugar; a teaspoon of stevia powder can replace a cup of sugar. It is, therefore, better to replace the sugar with keto sweeteners by adding them as per your taste.

Food to Eat

Dairy	Fruits	Vegetables	Meat	Nuts	Oils
Coconut milk	Avocados	Artichoke hearts	Beef	Almonds	Almond oil

Almond milk	Blueberries	Arugula	Chicken	Brazil nuts	Avocado oil
Coconut cream	Coconuts	Asparagus	Pork	Hazelnuts/filberts	Cacao butter
butter	Cranberries	Bell peppers	Fish	Macadamia nuts	Coconut oil
Cheeses	Lemons	Beets	Turkey	Pecans	Flaxseed oil
Silken Tofu	Limes	Bok choy	Duck	Peanuts	Hazelnut oil
ghee	Olives	Broccoli	Quail	Pine nuts	Macadamia nut oil
	Raspberries	Brussels sprouts	Shrimp	Walnuts	MCT oil
	Strawberries	Cabbage	Lobsters	Chia	Olive oil
	Tomatoes	Carrots	Mussels	Hemp	Healthy Oils
		Cauliflower	Prawns	Pumpkin	Almond oil

Chapter 4: Foods to Avoid

The main goal of a ketogenic diet is to minimize the carb intake, and it takes aversion from all such food products which have high carb profile. These are listed below:

1. Legumes

Legumes like all beans, lentils, and chickpeas, etc. are the underground parts of the plants where they store most of the food in the form of carbohydrates. Therefore, none of the legumes are keto friendly, and they all should be completely avoided on this diet.

2. Grains

All Edible grains are a good source of carbohydrates, like rice, wheat, millet, barley, etc. Grains are therefore strictly forbidden on a ketogenic diet. Food products obtained and processed from these grains are also not allowed like all-purpose flour, wheat flour, rice flours, chickpea flour, etc. The high carb grain flours can be replaced with:

1. Coconut flour

2. Almond flour

3. Fruits

Fruits including oranges, banana, apples, pineapple, pomegranate, pears, and watermelon are all very rich in sugars. Do not use these fruits on a ketogenic diet. All the Extracts and juices of these fruits should also be avoided.

4. Sugar

All sugars are carbohydrates whether its glucose, fructose, or maltose. Therefore, sugars should be avoided completely, including white sugar, granulated, confectionary, baking, brown sugar, etc. Products containing high dose of sugar are also not allowed like processed food and beverages.

5. Tubers

Tubers are including most of the underground vegetables like potatoes, beetroots, yellow squash, and yams. They all are not good for a ketogenic diet as they contain a high amount of starch, meaning carbohydrates.

6. Dairy

Animal milk, including cow, and goat milk is completely prohibited on this diet.

7. Sauces and Syrups

Ketchup, maple syrup, chocolate syrups, dates molasses, honey, etc. which contain sugars in high amount are also prohibited on a ketogenic diet. Replace the ketchup with a sugar-free one and use sugar-free chocolates for the recipes.

Dairy Products	Tubers /vegetables	Fruits	Legumes	Sugars	Grains
Animal Milk	Yams	Apples	Lentils	White	Rice
	Potatoes	Banana	Chickpeas	Brown	Wheat
	Beets	Pineapples	Black beans	Maple syrup	Corn
		Oranges	Garbanzo beans	Agave	Barley
		Pears	Lima Beans	Honey, Molasses	Millet
		Pomegranate	Kidney beans	Confectioner's sugar	Oats
		Watermelon	White beans	Granulated sugar	Quinoa

Chapter 5: FAQs

Q1. How ketogenic diets help to achieve weight loss?

This weight loss is achieved when the body undergoes ketosis. Ketogenic diet help to create an environment viable for ketosis; it reduces carbohydrates and provides fat-based meals. In such condition, the energy needs are met by the breakdown of accumulated body fats, and hence, weight loss is achieved.

Q2. Do we need to measure the level of ketones?

Testing the level of ketones in the body is only necessary for those who are not keto-adapted. When the body becomes used to of the new diet, and it adjusts itself according to it, there is no need to constantly measure the ketone levels.

Q3. What is Keto Adaption?

Whenever a person adopts a ketogenic diet, he undergoes progressive changes. There are three stages of change. The first is the initial phase, where you incorporate the ketogenic practices in your life. Then comes the adjustment phase, the crucial of all where the body learns to adjust itself to the new diet. it is also known as the keto adaption stages where you can witness the visible signs of ketosis. In the last phase, the person emerges as keto-adapted.

Q4. What is insulin, and what is its function?

Insulin is a vital hormone in the human body, which can help in regulating the blood glucose levels. Insulin aids the removal of glucose from the blood and directs it to the organs, whereas glucagon hormone works in contrast to Insulin and help the release of glucose into the blood. When the cells producing insulin are damaged, the blood glucose levels rise, which causes diabetes, and that can even lead to retardation, organ damage and blindness, etc.

Q5. Should I count calories intake? Does it really matter?

Caloric intake does matter, especially when you aiming to lose your weight. Low carb can surely guarantee weight loss, but control on caloric intake is also needed to limit the energy consumption. Calculate the overall calories per meal and also measure the amount of each macronutrient in the meal.

Chapter 6: 30 Days Meal Plan

Day 1

Breakfast: Cucumber Smoothie

Lunch: Cheesy Beef Burgers

Dinner: Braised Lamb Shanks

Snack: Baked Chicken Wings

Dessert: Chilled Lemony Treat

Day 2

Breakfast: Stuffed Avocados

Lunch: Asparagus Soup

Dinner: Bacon Wrapped Turkey Breast

Snack: Cheese Balls

Dessert: Vanilla Crème Brûlée

Day 3

Breakfast: Coconut Porridge

Lunch: Lemony Crab Legs

Dinner: Beef Stroganoff

Snack: Cucumber Cups

Dessert: Lemon Soufflé

Day 4

Breakfast: Salmon Scramble

Lunch: Creamy Brussels Sprout

Dinner: Parmesan Pork Chops

Snack: Avocado Salsa

Dessert: Chocolate Pudding

Day 5

Breakfast: Cream Cheese Waffles

Lunch: Spicy Ground Turkey

Dinner: Steak with Blueberry Sauce

Snack: Chicken Popcorn

Dessert: Chocolate Lava Cake

Day 6

Breakfast: Eggs with Cheese

Lunch: Broccoli Stir Fry

Dinner: Salmon Soup

Snack: Roasted Pumpkin Seeds

Dessert: Spinach Sorbet

Day 7

Breakfast: Cream Crepes

Lunch: Shrimp with Zucchini

Dinner: Chicken Parmigiana

Snack: Deviled Eggs

Dessert: Avocado Mousse

Day 8

Breakfast: Bacon Omelet

Lunch: Broccoli Stir Fry

Dinner: Stuffed Pork Chops

Snack: Bacon Wrapped Scallops

Dessert: Mocha Ice Cream

Day 9

Breakfast: Cottage Cheese Pancakes

Lunch: Parmesan Halibut

Dinner: Butter Chicken

Snack: Mini Mushroom Pizza

Dessert: Ricotta Mousse

Day 10

Breakfast: Cheddar Omelet

Lunch: Buttered Scallops

Dinner: Lamb Chops in Garlic Sauce

Snack: Avocado Gazpacho

Dessert: Pumpkin Custard

Day 11

Breakfast: Cucumber Smoothie

Lunch: Broccoli Soup

Dinner: Salmon with Cream Cheese

Snack: Baked Chicken Wings

Dessert: Chilled Lemony Treat

Day 12

Breakfast: Stuffed Avocados

Lunch: Cheesy Beef Burgers

Dinner: Roasted Trout

Snack: Cheese Balls

Dessert: Vanilla Crème Brûlée

Day 13

Breakfast: Coconut Porridge

Lunch: Spicy Mushrooms

Dinner: Stuffed Chicken Breast

Snack: Cucumber Cups

Dessert: Lemon Soufflé

Day 14

Breakfast: Salmon Scramble

Lunch: Creamy Brussels Sprout

Dinner: Chicken with Cranberries

Snack: Avocado Salsa

Dessert: Chocolate Pudding

Day 15

Breakfast: Cream Cheese Waffles

Lunch: Shrimp with Zucchini

Dinner: Chicken Soup

Snack: Chicken Popcorn

Dessert: Chocolate Lava Cake

Day 16

Breakfast: Eggs with Cheese

Lunch: Broccoli Soup

Dinner: Cod in Butter Sauce

Snack: Roasted Pumpkin Seeds

Dessert: Spinach Sorbet

Day 17

Breakfast: Cream Crepes

Lunch: Prawns in Mushroom Sauce

Dinner: Baked Chicken Legs

Snack: Deviled Eggs

Dessert: Avocado Mousse

Day 18

Breakfast: Bacon Omelet

Lunch: Cheesy Spinach

Dinner: Cheese & Walnut Coated Lamb Chops

Snack: Bacon Wrapped Scallops

Dessert: Mocha Ice Cream

Day 19

Breakfast: Cottage Cheese Pancakes

Lunch: Spicy Ground Turkey

Dinner: Cod in Butter Sauce

Snack: Mini Mushroom Pizza

Dessert: Ricotta Mousse

Day 20

Breakfast: Cheddar Omelet

Lunch: Prawns in Mushroom Sauce

Dinner: Parmesan Chicken

Snack: Avocado Gazpacho

Dessert: Pumpkin Custard

Day 21

Breakfast: Cucumber Smoothie

Lunch: Broccoli Stir Fry

Dinner: Cheesy Pork Cutlets

Snack: Baked Chicken Wings

Dessert: Chilled Lemony Treat

Day 22

Breakfast: Stuffed Avocados

Lunch: Scallops with Broccoli

Dinner: Steak with Blueberry Sauce

Snack: Cheese Balls

Dessert: Vanilla Crème Brûlée

Day 23

Breakfast: Coconut Porridge

Lunch: Cheesy Spinach

Dinner: Beef Stroganoff

Snack: Cucumber Cups

Dessert: Lemon Soufflé

Day 24

Breakfast: Salmon Scramble

Lunch: Roasted Lamb Chops

Dinner: Chicken Soup

Snack: Avocado Salsa

Dessert: Chocolate Pudding

Day 25

Breakfast: Cream Cheese Waffles

Lunch: Lemony Crab Legs

Dinner: Braised Lamb Shanks

Snack: Chicken Popcorn

Dessert: Chocolate Lava Cake

Day 26

Breakfast: Eggs with Cheese

Lunch: Buttered Scallops

Dinner: Chicken in Capers Sauce

Snack: Roasted Pumpkin Seeds

Dessert: Spinach Sorbet

Day 27

Breakfast: Cream Crepes

Lunch: Spicy Mushrooms

Dinner: Lamb Chops in Garlic Sauce

Snack: Deviled Eggs

Dessert: Avocado Mousse

Day 28

Breakfast: Bacon Omelet

Lunch: Cheesy Beef Burgers

Dinner: Chicken with Spinach

Snack: Bacon Wrapped Scallops

Dessert: Mocha Ice Cream

Day 29

Breakfast: Cottage Cheese Pancakes

Lunch: Asparagus Soup

Dinner: Roasted Trout

Snack: Mini Mushroom Pizza

Dessert: Ricotta Mousse

Day 30

Breakfast: Cheddar Omelet

Lunch: Scallops with Broccoli

Dinner: Ground Beef Soup

Snack: Avocado Gazpacho

Dessert: Pumpkin Custard

Chapter 7: Breakfast Recipes

Cucumber Smoothie

Preparation Time: 10 minutes
Servings: 2

Ingredients:

- 1 small cucumber, peeled and chopped
- 1 cup mixed fresh greens (spinach, kale, beet greens), trimmed and chopped
- ½ cup lettuce, torn
- 4 tablespoons fresh parsley leaves
- 6-8 drops liquid stevia
- 1 teaspoon fresh lemon juice
- 2 cups chilled water

Method:

1. Add all the ingredients in a high-speed blender and pulse until smooth.
2. Pour the smoothie into serving glasses and serve.

Nutritional Value:

- Calories 30
- Total Fat 0.3 g
- Saturated Fat 0.1 g
- Cholesterol 0 mg
- Total Carbs 6.8 g
- Sugar 2.8 g
- Fiber 1.3 g
- Sodium 11 mg
- Potassium 286 mg
- Protein 1.5 g

Coconut Porridge

Preparation Time: 10 minutes
Cooking Time: 5 minutes
Servings: 2

Ingredients:

- ½ cup unsweetened coconut flakes
- ¼ cup hemp seeds
- 1 tablespoon coconut flour
- ½ cup water
- 1/3 cup unsweetened coconut milk
- 1 teaspoon organic vanilla extract
- 1-2 teaspoons monk fruit sweetener

Method:

1. In a pan, add the coconut, hemp seeds, water and coconut milk over medium heat and bring to boil, stirring frequently.
2. Simmer for about 2 minutes, stirring continuously.
3. Stir in the vanilla extract and sweetener and remove from the heat.
4. Serve immediately with your desired topping.

Nutritional Value:

- Calories 267
- Total Fat 22.8 g
- Saturated Fat 14.1 g
- Cholesterol 0 mg
- Total Carbs 10 g
- Sugar 1.6 g
- Fiber 4.9 g
- Sodium 8 mg
- Potassium 249 mg
- Protein 7.4

Cream Cheese Waffles

Preparation Time: 10 minutes
Cooking Time: 8 minutes
Servings: 2

Ingredients:

- 4 ounces cream cheese, softened
- 4 large organic eggs
- 6 tablespoons almond flour
- 2 tablespoon butter, melted
- 1 tablespoon powdered Erythritol
- 1 teaspoon organic baking powder

Method:

1. Preheat the waffle iron and then grease it.
2. Add all the ingredients in a blender and pulse until smooth.
3. Place half of the mixture into preheated waffle iron and cook for about 3-4 minutes or until golden brown.
4. Repeat with the remaining mixture.
5. Serve warm with your favorite topping.

Nutritional Value:

- Calories 569
- Total Fat 50.7 g
- Saturated Fat 23.3 g
- Cholesterol 464 mg
- Total Carbs 9 g
- Sugar 1.9 g
- Fiber 2.3 g
- Sodium 323 mg
- Potassium 454 mg
- Protein 22.4 g

Cottage Cheese Pancakes

Preparation Time: 10 minutes
Cooking Time: 12 minutes
Servings: 2

Ingredients:

- 7 ounces cottage cheese
- 2 organic eggs
- 1½ tablespoons psyllium husk

Method:

1. In a bowl, add all the ingredients and with a hand blender, mix until well combined.
2. Heat a greased skillet over me medium-low heat.
3. Add half of the mixture and tilt the pan to spread it in an even layer.
4. Cook for about 2-3 minutes.
5. Flip the side and cook for about 1-2 minutes or until golden brown
6. Repeat with the remaining butter and spinach mixture.
7. Serve warm with your favorite topping.

Nutritional Value:

- Calories 165
- Total Fat 6.3 g
- Saturated Fat 2.6 g
- Cholesterol 172 mg
- Total Carbs 7.7 g
- Sugar 0.7 g
- Fiber 3.4 g
- Sodium 468 mg
- Potassium 195 mg
- Protein 19.2 g

Cream Crepes

Preparation Time: 15 minutes
Cooking Time: 12 minutes
Servings: 2

Ingredients:

- 2 tablespoons coconut oil, melted and divided
- 2 organic eggs
- 1 teaspoon Splenda
- 1/8 teaspoon salt
- 2 tablespoons coconut flour
- 1/3 cup heavy cream

Method:

1. In a bowl, add 1 tablespoon of the oil, eggs, Splenda and salt and beat until well combined.
2. Slowly, add the flour, beating continuously until well combined.
3. Add the heavy cream and stir until well combined.
4. Grease a large non-stick skillet with the remaining oil and heat over medium heat.
5. Add ¼ of the mixture and tilt the pan to spread into a thin layer.
6. Cook for about 3 minutes, flipping once after 2 minutes.
7. Repeat with the remaining mixture.
8. Serve warm with your favorite topping.

Nutritional Value:

- Calories 289
- Total Fat 26.1 g
- Saturated Fat 18.2 g
- Cholesterol 191 mg
- Total Carbs 7.9 g
- Sugar 2.4 g
- Fiber 3 g
- Sodium 216 mg
- Potassium 74 mg
- Protein 7 g

Cheddar Bread

Preparation Time: 10 minutes
Cooking Time: 1½ minutes
Servings: 2

Ingredients:

- 2 tablespoons coconut flour
- 2½ tablespoons unsalted butter, melted
- 2 tablespoons cheddar cheese, grated
- 2 organic eggs
- 2 teaspoons sour cream
- ½ teaspoon organic baking powder

Method:

1. In a small bowl, add all the ingredients and beat until smooth.
2. Place the mixture into 2 greased 3x3-inch glass microwave-safe bowls evenly.
3. With the back of a spoon, press the mixture to smooth the top surface.
4. Microwave on High for about 90 seconds.
5. Remove from the microwave and set aside to cool for about 2-3 minutes.
6. Carefully, invert the breads onto a plate and serve.

Nutritional Value:

- Calories 258
- Total Fat 22.7 g
- Saturated Fat 13 g
- Cholesterol 211 mg
- Total Carbs 6.2 g
- Sugar 0.4 g
- Fiber 3 g
- Sodium 202 mg
- Potassium 331 mg
- Protein 8.6 g

Eggs with Cheese

Preparation Time: 15 minutes
Cooking Time: 6 minutes
Servings: 2

Ingredients:

- 4 organic eggs (whites and yolks separated)
- 4 tablespoons cooked bacon, crumbled
- 4 tablespoons fresh chives, chopped finely
- 4 tablespoons Pecorino-Romano cheese, grated
- Freshly ground black pepper, as required

Method:

1. Preheat the oven to 450 degrees F. Line a baking sheet with parchment paper.
2. In a bowl, add the egg whites and beat until stiff peaks form.
3. Add the bacon, chives and cheese and stir to combine.
4. With a tablespoon, place the mixture onto prepared baking sheet in 4 mounds.
5. With your finger, make a deep well in each mound.
6. Bake for about 3 minutes.
7. Remove the baking sheet from the oven.
8. Carefully, place 1 egg yolk in each well and sprinkle with black pepper.
9. Bake for about 2-3 minutes more.
10. Serve immediately.

Nutritional Value:

- *Calories 254*
- *Total Fat 18.6 g*
- *Saturated Fat 6.7 g*
- *Cholesterol 353 mg*
- *Total Carbs 1.2 g*

- *Sugar 0.8 g*
- *Fiber 0.2 g*
- *Sodium 203 mg*
- *Potassium 215 mg*
- *Protein 20.5 g*

Bacon Omelet

Preparation Time: 10 minutes
Cooking Time: 15 minutes
Servings: 2

Ingredients:

- 4 large organic eggs
- 1 tablespoon fresh chives, minced
- Salt and ground black pepper, as required
- 4 bacon slices
- 1 tablespoon unsalted butter
- 2 ounces Cheddar cheese, shredded

Method:

1. In a bowl, add the eggs, chives, salt and black pepper and beat until well combined.
2. Heat a non-stick frying pan over medium-high heat and cook the bacon slices for about 8-10 minutes.
3. Place the bacon onto a paper towel-lined plate to drain. Then chop the bacon slices.
4. With a paper towels, wipe out the frying pan.
5. In the same frying pan, melt the butter over medium-low heat and cook the egg mixture for about 2 minutes.
6. Carefully, flip the omelet and top with chopped bacon.
7. Cook for 1-2 minutes or until desired doneness of eggs.
8. Remove from heat and immediately, place the cheese in the center of omelet.
9. Fold the edges of omelet over cheese and cut into 2 portions.
10. Serve immediately.

Nutritional Value:

- *Calories 622*
- *Total Fat 49.3 g*
- *Saturated Fat 20.7 g*
- *Cholesterol 481 mg*
- *Total Carbs 2 g*
- *Sugar 1 g*
- *Fiber 0 g*
- *Sodium 1700 mg*
- *Potassium 331 mg*
- *Protein 41.2 g*

Salmon Scramble

Preparation Time: 15 minutes
Cooking Time: 5 minutes
Servings: 2

Ingredients:

- 4 organic eggs
- 2 organic egg yolks
- 2 tablespoons fresh dill, chopped finely
- ¼ teaspoon red pepper flakes, crushed
- ¼ teaspoon garlic powder
- Freshly ground black pepper, as required
- 4 smoked salmon pieces, chopped
- 2 tablespoons unsalted butter

Method:

1. In a bowl, add all the ingredients except salmon and butter and beat until well combined.
2. Stir in the chopped salmon.
3. In a frying pan, melt the butter over medium-low heat.
4. Add the egg mixture and cook for about 3-5 minutes or until done completely, stirring continuously.
5. Serve immediately.

Nutritional Value:

- Calories 358
- Total Fat 27.4 g
- Saturated Fat 12.2 g
- Cholesterol 581 mg
- Total Carbs 3.4 g
- Sugar 0.9 g
- Fiber 0.5 g
- Sodium 1300 mg
- Potassium 351 mg
- Protein 25 g

Stuffed Avocados

Preparation Time: 15 minutes
Cooking Time: 15 minutes
Servings: 2

Ingredients:

- 1 ripe avocado, halved lengthwise and pitted
- 1 teaspoon garlic powder
- 2 medium organic eggs
- Salt and ground black pepper, as required
- 1 tablespoon Parmesan cheese, shredded
- ½ teaspoon fresh chives, minced

Method:

1. Preheat the oven to 350 degrees F. Line a small baking sheet with a piece of foil.
2. Carefully, scoop out 1-2 tablespoons of flesh from the center of each avocado half.
3. Arrange avocado halves onto the prepared baking sheet, cut side up.
4. Sprinkle each avocado half with the garlic powder evenly.
5. Carefully, crack one egg into each avocado half.
6. Sprinkle each egg with salt and black pepper and then, top evenly with the cheese.
7. Bake for about 12-15 minutes or until desired doneness of the egg whites.
8. Remove from the oven and set aside to cool slightly.
9. Garnish with fresh chives and serve warm.

Nutritional Value:

- *Calories 283*
- *Total Fat 24.7 g*
- *Saturated Fat 5.9 g*
- *Cholesterol 165 mg*
- *Total Carbs 10 g*
- *Sugar 1.2 g*
- *Fiber 6.9 g*
- *Sodium 188 mg*
- *Potassium 565 mg*
- *Protein 8.7 g*

Chapter 8: Appetizer & Snacks Recipes

Avocado Gazpacho

Preparation Time: 15 minutes
Servings: 2

Ingredients:

- 2 avocados, peeled, pitted and chopped
- 3 tablespoons fresh cilantro leaves
- 1½ cups homemade vegetable broth
- 1 tablespoon fresh lemon juice
- ½ teaspoon ground cumin
- 1/8 teaspoon cayenne pepper
- Salt, as required

Method:

1. Add all the ingredients in a high-speed blender and pulse until smooth.
2. Transfer the gazpacho into a large bowl.
3. Cover the bowl and refrigerate to chill completely before serving.

Nutritional Value:

- Calories 235
- Total Fat 20.7 g
- Saturated Fat 4.4 g
- Cholesterol 0 mg
- Total Carbs 9.4 g
- Sugar 1 g
- Fiber 6.8 g
- Sodium 657 mg
- Potassium 652 mg
- Protein 5.6 g

Cucumber Cups

Preparation Time: 15 minutes
Servings: 2

Ingredients:

- 4 ounces cooked salmon, very finely chopped
- 2 tablespoons heavy cream
- ½ tablespoon shallots, minced
- ½ tablespoon fresh chives, minced
- 1/8 teaspoon smoked paprika
- Salt and ground black pepper, as required
- ½ English cucumber, peeled and cut crosswise into ¾-inch thick slices

Method:

1. Add all the ingredients except cucumber in a bowl and mix until well combined.
2. With a teaspoon, scoop out the center of each cucumber slice slightly.
3. Place the salmon mixture over each cucumber slice and serve immediately.

Nutritional Value:

- *Calories 140*
- *Total Fat 9.2 g*
- *Saturated Fat 4 g*
- *Cholesterol 46 mg*
- *Total Carbs 3.7 g*
- *Sugar 1.3 g*
- *Fiber 0.5 g*
- *Sodium 110 mg*
- *Potassium 353 mg*
- *Protein 11.9 g*

Mini Mushroom Pizzas

Preparation Time: 15 minutes
Cooking Time: 25 minutes
Servings: 2

Ingredients:

- 2 large Portobello mushrooms, stems removed
- ¼ cup sugar-free marinara sauce
- ¼ cup mozzarella cheese, shredded
- ½ gluten-free chorizo link, cut into thin slices

Method:

1. Preheat the oven to 375 degrees F. Line a medium baking sheet with a lightly greased parchment paper.
2. With a spoon, scrape out the dark gills from mushrooms and discard the gills.
3. Arrange the mushrooms onto prepared baking sheet, stem side up.
4. Top each mushroom with the marinara sauce, followed by the mozzarella cheese and chorizo slices.
5. Bake for about 20-25 minutes or until the cheese is bubbly.
6. Remove from the oven and serve immediately.

Nutritional Value:

- Calories 106
- Total Fat 6.4 g
- Saturated Fat 2.5 g
- Cholesterol 15 mg
- Total Carbs 4.9 g
- Sugar 1 g
- Fiber 1.5 g
- Sodium 299 mg
- Potassium 360 mg
- Protein 8.1 g

Cheese Balls

Preparation Time: 15 minutes
Cooking Time: 12 minutes
Servings: 2

Ingredients:

- 1 organic egg
- ¼ cup cheddar cheese, shredded
- 2 tablespoons Parmesan cheese, shredded
- 2 tablespoons mozzarella cheese, shredded
- ¼ cup almond flour
- ¼ teaspoon organic baking powder
- Ground black pepper, as required

Method:

1. Preheat oven to 400 degrees F. Line a baking sheet with parchment paper.
2. Crack the egg into a bowl and beat lightly.
3. Now, place the remaining ingredients and mix until well combined.
4. Make 4 equal-sized balls from the mixture.
5. Arrange the balls onto the prepared baking sheet in a single layer.
6. Bake for about 10-12 minutes or until golden brown.
7. Remove from the oven and transfer the cheese balls onto a platter.
8. Set aside to cool slightly before serving.

Nutritional Value:

- Calories 274
- Total Fat 19.9 g
- Saturated Fat 8 g
- Cholesterol 115 mg
- Total Carbs 4.9 g
- Sugar 0.2 g
- Fiber 1.5 g
- Sodium 379 mg
- Potassium 112 mg
- Protein 19.2 g

Bacon Wrapped Scallops

Preparation Time: 10 minutes
Cooking Time: 15 minutes
Servings: 2

Ingredients:

- 4 sea scallops, side muscles removed
- 2 bacon slices, cut in half crosswise
- ½ teaspoons olive oil
- Salt and ground black pepper, as required

Method:

1. Preheat the oven to 425 degrees F. Line a baking sheet with parchment paper.
2. Wrap each scallop with 1 bacon slice half and secure with the toothpicks.
3. Drizzle the scallops with the oil evenly and then, season with salt and black pepper.
4. Arrange the scallops onto the prepared baking sheet in a single layer.
5. Bake for about 12-15 minutes or until scallop is tender and opaque.
6. Remove from the oven and serve immediately.

Nutritional Value:

- *Calories 220*
- *Total Fat 13.8 g*
- *Saturated Fat 4.2 g*
- *Cholesterol 52 mg*
- *Total Carbs 1.8 g*

- *Sugar 0 g*
- *Fiber 0 g*
- *Sodium 203 mg*
- *Potassium 357 mg*
- *Protein 20.8 g*

Baked Chicken Wings

Preparation Time: 15 minutes
Cooking Time: 50 minutes
Servings: 2

Ingredients:

- 1-pound grass-fed chicken wings
- ¼ cup mayonnaise
- 2½ ounces Parmesan cheese, grated
- 1 tablespoon garlic & herb seasoning blend

Method:

1. Preheat the oven to 375 degrees F. Line a baking sheet pan with a piece of foil.
2. Cut each chicken wing into three parts (wing, drumettes and tip).
3. With paper towels, pat the wings dry completely.
4. In a bowl, add the chicken wings and mayonnaise and mix well.
5. Ina shallow bowl, add the Parmesan cheese and seasoning blend and mix well.
6. Coat each chicken wing piece with the Parmesan cheese mixture evenly.
7. Arrange the chicken wing pieces onto the prepared baking sheet in a single layer.
8. Bake for about 40-50 minutes or until golden brown.
9. Remove from the oven and serve immediately.

Nutritional Value:

- *Calories 700*
- *Total Fat 44.4 g*
- *Saturated Fat 12.7 g*
- *Cholesterol 237 mg*
- *Total Carbs 2.8 g*
- *Sugar 0 g*
- *Fiber 0.5 g*
- *Sodium 889 mg*
- *Potassium 551 mg*
- *Protein 77 g*

Avocado Salsa

Preparation Time: 15 minutes
Servings: 2

Ingredients:

- 1 ripe avocado, peeled, pitted and chopped
- ½ cup tomato, chopped
- 2 tablespoons onion, chopped
- 2 tablespoons fresh cilantro, minced
- 1 tablespoon olive oil
- 1 tablespoon fresh lime juice
- Salt and ground black pepper, as required

Method:

1. In a large serving bowl, add all the ingredients and gently, stir to combine.
2. With a plastic wrap, cover the bowl and refrigerate before serving.

Nutritional Value:

- *Calories 278*
- *Total Fat 26.7 g*
- *Saturated Fat 5.1 g*
- *Cholesterol 0 mg*
- *Total Carbs 11 g*
- *Sugar 2.1 g*
- *Fiber 7.5 g*
- *Sodium 87 mg*
- *Potassium 614 mg*
- *Protein 2.4 g*

Roasted Pumpkin Seeds

Preparation Time: 10 minutes
Cooking Time: 20 minutes
Servings: 2

Ingredients:

- ½ cup pumpkin seeds, washed and dried
- 1 teaspoon garam masala
- 1/8 teaspoon red chili powder
- 1/8 teaspoon ground turmeric
- Salt, as required
- 1 tablespoons coconut oil, melted
- ¼ tablespoon fresh lemon juice

Method:

1. Preheat the oven to 350 degrees F. Lightly, grease a baking sheet.
2. Add all ingredients except lemon juice in a bowl and toss to coat well.
3. Transfer the pumpkin need mixture onto the prepared baking sheet.
4. Roast for about 20 minutes, flipping occasionally.
5. Remove from the oven and let it cool completely before serving.
6. Drizzle with lemon juice and serve.

Nutritional Value:

- Calories 247
- Total Fat 22.7 g
- Saturated Fat 8.9 g
- Cholesterol 0 mg
- Total Carbs 6.4 g
- Sugar 1.4 g
- Fiber 0.4 g
- Sodium 88 mg
- Potassium 287 mg
- Protein 8.5 g

Spinach Chips

Preparation Time: 10 minutes
Cooking Time: 8 minutes
Servings: 2

Ingredients:

- 3 cups fresh spinach leaves
- 1/8 teaspoon cayenne pepper
- Salt, as required
- ½ tablespoon olive oil

Method:

1. Preheat the oven to 325 degrees F. Line a large baking sheet with a parchment paper.
2. Arrange the spinach leaves onto the prepared baking sheet in a single layer.
3. Sprinkle the kale with cayenne pepper and salt and drizzle with oil.
4. Bake for about 8 minutes.
5. Remove from the oven and set aside to cool before serving.

Nutritional Value:

- Calories 41
- Total Fat 3.7 g
- Saturated Fat 0.5 g
- Cholesterol 0 mg
- Total Carbs 1.7 g
- Sugar 0.2 g
- Fiber 4 g
- Sodium 1 mg
- Potassium 253 mg
- Protein 1.3 g

Deviled Eggs

Preparation Time: 15 minutes
Cooking Time: 15 minutes
Servings: 2

Ingredients:

- 2 large organic eggs
- 1 cooked bacon strip, crumbled
- 1 tablespoon sour cream
- 1 tablespoon sharp cheddar cheese shredded
- 1 teaspoon fresh chive, minced
- 1/8 teaspoons Dijon mustard
- Pinch of garlic powder
- Pinch of salt and ground black pepper
- Pinch of paprika

Method:

1. In a pan of the boiling water, place the eggs and again bring to a boil over high heat.
2. Reduce the heat to low and cook, covered for about 12 minutes.
3. Remove from the heat and drain the eggs completely.
4. Set the eggs aside to cool completely.
5. Peel the eggs and then cut in half lengthwise.
6. Remove the egg yolks and place in a bowl.
7. With a fork, mash the egg yolks.
8. Add the remaining ingredients except paprika and stir to combine.
9. Place the mixture in each egg white half evenly and sprinkle with the paprika.
10. Arrange the eggs onto a plate.
11. Cover the plate and refrigerate to chill before serving.

Nutritional Value:

- *Calories 178*
- *Total Fat 13.4 g*
- *Saturated Fat 5.1 g*
- *Cholesterol 208 mg*
- *Total Carbs 1.2 g*
- *Sugar 0.5 g*

- Fiber 0.1 g
- Sodium 434 mg
- Potassium 165 mg
- Protein 12.7 g

Chicken Popcorn

Preparation Time: 15 minutes
Cooking Time: 25 minutes
Servings: 2

Ingredients:

- ½ pound grass-fed chicken thigh, cut into bite-sized pieces
- 7 ounces unsweetened coconut milk
- 1 teaspoon ground turmeric
- Salt and ground black pepper, as required
- 2 tablespoons coconut flour
- 3 tablespoons desiccated coconut
- 1 tablespoon unsalted butter, melted

Method:

1. Add the chicken, coconut milk, turmeric, salt and black pepper in a large bowl and mix well.
2. Cover and refrigerate to marinate overnight.
3. Preheat the oven to 390 degrees F. Line a baking sheet with parchment paper.
4. In a shallow dish, add the coconut flour and desiccated coconut and mix well.
5. Coat the chicken pieces with the coconut mixture evenly.
6. Arrange the chicken piece onto the prepared baking sheet and drizzle with the melted butter evenly.
7. Bake for about 20-25 minutes.
8. Remove from the oven and serve immediately.

Nutritional Value:

- *Calories 345*
- *Total Fat 19.2 g*
- *Saturated Fat 10.4 g*
- *Cholesterol 116 mg*
- *Total Carbs 7.7 g*
- *Sugar 0.5 g*
- *Fiber 4.3 g*
- *Sodium 218 mg*
- *Potassium 348 mg*
- *Protein 34.2 g*

Onion Rings

Preparation Time: 15 minutes
Cooking Time: 15 minutes
Servings: 2

Ingredients:

- 1 medium yellow onion, cut into ½-inch thick rings
- ½ cup coconut flour
- 1 tablespoon heavy whipping cream
- 2 large organic eggs
- ½ cup Parmesan cheese, grated
- 2 ounces pork rinds

Method:

1. Preheat the oven to 425 degrees F. Arrange a greased rack onto a large baking sheet.
2. Break apart the onion rings and discard inside pieces.
3. In a shallow bowl, place the coconut flour.
4. In a second shallow bowl, add the heavy cream and egg and beat until well combined.
5. In a third shallow bowl, mix together the Parmesan cheese and pork rinds.
6. Coat each onion ring with the coconut flour, then dip into the egg mixture and finally, coat with the cheese mixture.
7. Repeat the procedure of coating once.
8. Arrange the coated onion rings onto the prepared rack in a single layer.
9. Bake for about 15 minutes.
10. Remove from the oven and serve warm.

Nutritional Value:

- Calories 368
- Total Fat 23.2 g
- Saturated Fat 10.2 g
- Cholesterol 253 mg
- Total Carbs 7.7 g
- Sugar 3 g
- Fiber 2.4 g
- Sodium 801 mg
- Potassium 153 mg
- Protein 33.8 g

Chapter 9: Beef, Pork & Lamb Recipes

Beef Stroganoff

Preparation Time: 15 minutes
Cooking Time: 22 minutes
Servings: 2

Ingredients:

For Mushroom Gravy:

- 2 bacon slices, chopped
- 1½ tablespoons butter
- 1 garlic clove, minced
- ½ teaspoon dried thyme
- ¾ cup fresh button mushrooms, sliced
- Salt and ground black pepper, as required
- 3½ ounces cream cheese, softened
- ¼ cup heavy cream

For Steak:

- 2 (6-ounce) grass-fed beef tenderloin fillets
- Salt and ground black pepper, as required
- 1½ tablespoons butter

Method:

1. For mushroom gravy: heat a large nonstick skillet over medium-high heat and cook the bacon for about 8-10 minutes.
2. With a slotted spoon, transfer the bacon onto a paper towel-lined plate to drain.
3. Discard the bacon grease from skillet.
4. In the same skillet, melt the butter over medium heat and sauté the garlic and thyme for about 1 minute.
5. Stir in the mushrooms, salt, and black pepper and cook for about 5-7 minutes, stirring frequently.
6. Reduce the heat to low and stir in the cream cheese until smooth.

7. Stir in the cream and cook for about 2-3 minutes or until heated completely.
8. Meanwhile, rub the beef fillets with salt and black pepper evenly.
9. In a large cast iron skillet, melt the butter over medium heat and cook the filets for about 5-7 minutes per side.
10. Remove the skillet of mushroom gravy from heat and stir in the bacon.
11. Place the filets onto serving plates and serve with the topping of mushroom gravy.

Nutritional Value:

- *Calories 814*
- *Total Fat 64.4 g*
- *Saturated Fat 33.8 g*
- *Cholesterol 273 mg*
- *Total Carbs 3.7 g*

- *Sugar 0.6 g*
- *Fiber 0.4 g*
- *Sodium 1105 mg*
- *Potassium 331 mg*
- *Protein 53.6 g*

Steak with Cream Sauce

Preparation Time: 15 minutes
Cooking Time: 55 minutes
Servings: 2

Ingredients:

- 2 cups heavy cream
- Pinch of onion powder
- Pinch of garlic powder
- Pinch of lemon pepper
- Salt and ground black pepper, as required
- 2 (8-ounce) grass-fed beef tenderloin steaks
- 1½ ounces Gorgonzola cheese, crumbled
- 1½ tablespoons Parmesan cheese, shredded
- Pinch of ground nutmeg

Method:

1. In a pan, add the heavy cream over medium heat and bring to a boil.
2. Reduce the heat to low and cook for about 40-50 minutes, stirring occasionally.
3. Meanwhile, preheat the outdoor grill to medium-high heat. Grease the grill grate.
4. In a small bowl, mix together onion powder, garlic powder, lemon pepper, salt and black pepper.
5. Sprinkle the steaks with seasoning mixture evenly.
6. Grill the steaks for about 4-5 minutes from both sides or until desired doneness.
7. Remove the pan of cream from heat and immediately, stir in the cheeses, nutmeg, salt and black pepper until well combined.
8. Place the steaks onto serving plates and top with the creamy sauce evenly.
9. Serve immediately.

Nutritional Value:

- *Calories 961*
- *Total Fat 81.2 g*
- *Saturated Fat 44.1 g*
- *Cholesterol 327 mg*
- *Total Carbs 5.1 g*
- *Sugar 0.3 g*
- *Fiber 0.7 g*
- *Sodium 504 mg*
- *Potassium 97 mg*
- *Protein 54.3 g*

Steak with Blueberry Sauce

Preparation Time: 15 minutes
Cooking Time: 15 minutes
Servings: 2

Ingredients:

For Sauce:

- 1 tablespoon butter
- 1 tablespoon yellow onion, chopped
- 1 garlic clove, minced
- ½ teaspoon fresh thyme, chopped finely
- 1¼ cups homemade beef broth
- 1 tablespoon fresh lemon juice
- 1/3 cup fresh blueberries

For Steak:

- 1 tablespoon butter
- 2 (6-ounce) grass-fed flank steaks
- Salt and ground black pepper, as required

Method:

1. For sauce: in a pan, melt the butter over medium heat and sauté the onion for about 2 minutes.
2. Add the garlic and thyme and sauté for about 1 minute.
3. Stir in the broth and bring to a gentle simmer.
4. Reduce the heat to low and cook for about 10 minutes.
5. Meanwhile, for steak: in a skillet, melt the butter over medium-high heat and cook steaks with salt and black pepper for about 3-4 minutes per side.
6. With a slotted spoon, transfer the steak onto the serving plates.
7. Add the sauce in the skillet and stir to scrape up the brown bits from the bottom.
8. Stir in the lemon juice, blueberries, salt and black pepper and cook for about 1-2 minutes.
9. Remove from the heat and place the blueberry sauce over the steaks.

10. Serve immediately.

Nutritional Value:

- Calories 476
- Total Fat 26.7 g
- Saturated Fat 13.5 g
- Cholesterol 124 mg
- Total Carbs 5.4 g

- Sugar 3.2 g
- Fiber 0.8 g
- Sodium 734 mg
- Potassium 751 mg
- Protein 50.9 g

Cheesy Beef Burgers

Preparation Time: 15 minutes
Cooking Time: 5 minutes
Servings: 2

Ingredients:

- 8 ounces grass-fed lean ground beef
- Salt and ground black pepper, as required
- 1-ounce mozzarella cheese, cubed
- 1 tablespoon butter
- 2 ounces cheddar cheese, sliced
- 2 cooked bacon slices, chopped

Method:

1. In a bowl, add all the ingredients except butter and cheese and mix until well combined.
2. Make 2 equal sized patties from the mixture.
3. Place the mozzarella cubes inside of each patty and cover with the beef.
4. In a frying pan, melt the butter over medium heat and cook the patties for about 2-3 minutes.
5. Carefully, flip the side and top each patty with cheese evenly.
6. Cook for about 1-2 minutes.
7. Serve hot with the topping of bacon.

Nutritional Value:

- Calories 573
- Total Fat 36.9 g
- Saturated Fat 17.8 g
- Cholesterol 186 mg
- Total Carbs 1.3 g
- Sugar 0.2 g
- Fiber 0 g
- Sodium 1120 mg
- Potassium 650 mg
- Protein 56.3 g

Pork in Creamy Sauce

Preparation Time: 15 minutes
Cooking Time: 20 minutes
Servings: 2

Ingredients:

For Pork Loin:

- 1 teaspoon dried thyme
- 1 teaspoon paprika
- Salt and ground black pepper, as required
- 4 (4-ounce) pork loins

For Sauce:

- ½ cup homemade chicken broth
- ¼ cup heavy cream
- 1 teaspoon organic apple cider vinegar
- 1 tablespoon fresh lemon juice
- 1 tablespoon mustard
- 2 tablespoons fresh parsley, chopped

Method:

1. In a small bowl, mix together the thyme, paprika, salt, and black pepper.
2. Coat each pork loin evenly with the thyme mixture.
3. Heat a lightly greased large pan over high heat and sear the pork loins for about 2-3 minutes per side.
4. With a slotted spoon, transfer the pork loins onto a plate.
5. In the same pan, add the broth, heavy cream, and vinegar over medium heat and bring to a gentle simmer.
6. Add the lemon juice, and mustard and stir to combine.
7. Stir in the cooked pork loins and simmer, covered partially for about 10 minutes.
8. Garnish with parsley and serve hot.

Nutritional Value:

- Calories 645
- Total Fat 39.3 g
- Saturated Fat 15.6 g
- Cholesterol 1202 mg
- Total Carbs 3.9 g

- Sugar 0.9 g
- Fiber 1.6 g
- Sodium 419 mg
- Potassium 1120 mg
- Protein 65.3 g

Cheesy Pork Cutlets

Preparation Time: 15 minutes
Cooking Time: 10 minutes
Servings: 2

Ingredients:

- 2 tablespoons Italian dressing
- 2 tablespoons Parmesan cheese, grated
- 1 teaspoon pork seasoning
- 2 (6-ounce) pork cutlets
- 1 tablespoons butter, divided

Method:

1. In a shallow dish, place the Italian dressing.
2. In another shallow dish, add the cheese and seasoning and mix well.
3. Dip each pork cutlet in Italian dressing and then, coat with the Parmesan mixture.
4. In a large wok, melt the butter over medium heat and cook the cutlets for about 5 minutes per side.
5. Serve hot.

Nutritional Value:

- Calories 397
- Total Fat 19.9 g
- Saturated Fat 8.9 g
- Cholesterol 164 mg
- Total Carbs 2.5 g

- Sugar 1.2 g
- Fiber 0 g
- Sodium 522 mg
- Potassium 725 mg
- Protein 50.6 g

Parmesan Pork Chops

Preparation Time: 15 minutes
Cooking Time: 25 minutes
Servings: 2

Ingredients:

- 1/3 cup Parmesan cheese, shredded
- 2 tablespoons butter, melted
- 3 garlic cloves, minced
- ¼ tablespoon fresh thyme, minced
- ¼ tablespoon fresh parsley, minced
- Salt and ground black pepper, as required
- 4 (3-ounce) center-cut thin boneless pork chops

Method:

1. Preheat the oven to 400 degrees F. Line a baking dish with a greased parchment paper.
2. In a bowl, mix together the cheese, butter, garlic, herbs, salt, and black pepper
3. Coat the chops with parmesan mixture evenly.
4. Arrange the pork chops into the prepared baking dish in a single layer.
5. Bake for about 20-25 minutes.
6. Remove the baking dish from oven and set the oven to broiler.
7. Broil the chops for about 3 minutes.
8. Remove from the oven and serve hot.

Nutritional Value:

- *Calories 408*
- *Total Fat 21.2 g*
- *Saturated Fat 11.7 g*
- *Cholesterol 164 mg*
- *Total Carbs 2.2 g*
- *Sugar 0.1 g*
- *Fiber 0.2 g*
- *Sodium 756 mg*
- *Potassium 50 mg*
- *Protein 7.9 g*

Stuffed Pork Chops

Preparation Time: 15 minutes
Cooking Time: 1 hour 5 minutes
Servings: 2

Ingredients:

- 2 bacon slices, chopped
- 2 (6-ounces) boneless pork chops
- 1½ ounces feta cheese, crumbled
- 1½ ounces blue cheese, crumbled
- 1-ounce cream cheese
- 2 medium scallions, chopped
- Salt and ground black pepper, as required

Method:

1. Preheat the oven to 350 degrees F. Grease a baking dish.
2. Heat a wok over medium-high heat and cook the bacon for about 6-7 minutes.
3. With a slotted spoon, transfer the bacon into a bowl, leaving the grease in wok.
4. In the bowl of bacon, add the feta cheese, blue cheese, cream cheese and scallion and mix well.
5. With a sharp knife, cut a slit into each pork chop horizontally, making a pocket for the filling.
6. Stuff each pork chop with the cheese mixture and then, secure with the toothpicks.
7. Rub the outside of pork chops with salt and black pepper.
8. Heat the same wok with bacon grease over high heat and sear the pork chops for about 1½ minutes per side.
9. Remove from the heat and arrange the chops into the prepared baking dish in a single layer.
10. Bake for about 55 minutes or until desired doneness.
11. Remove from oven and set the pork chops aside for about 3-5 minutes before serving.

Nutritional Value:

- *Calories 586*
- *Total Fat 33.7 g*

- Saturated Fat 16.3 g
- Cholesterol 207 mg
- Total Carbs 3.3 g
- Sugar 1.4 g

- Fiber 0.4 g
- Sodium 1400 mg
- Potassium 1006 mg
- Protein 64.2 g

Roasted Lamb Chops

Preparation Time: 15 minutes
Cooking Time: 16 minutes
Servings: 2

Ingredients:

- 2 teaspoons butter
- 4 (4-ounce) grass-fed lamb loin chops, trimmed
- Salt and ground black pepper, as required
- 2 tablespoons Parmesan cheese, shredded

Method:

1. Preheat the oven to 375 degrees F.
2. In a large oven-proof skillet, melt the butter over medium-high heat and sear the chops with salt and black pepper for about 1½-2 minutes per side.
3. Remove from the oven and transfer the skillet into the oven.
4. Roast for about 8-12 minutes.
5. Serve hot with the sprinkling of the Parmesan.

Nutritional Value:

- *Calories 476*
- *Total Fat 21.8 g*
- *Saturated Fat 9.2 g*
- *Cholesterol 2168 mg*
- *Total Carbs 0.2 g*
- *Sugar 0 g*
- *Fiber 0 g*
- *Sodium 284 mg*
- *Potassium 331 mg*
- *Protein 65.6 g*

Lamb Chops in Garlic Sauce

Preparation Time: 15 minutes
Cooking Time: 10 minutes
Servings: 2

Ingredients:

- 1½ tablespoons butter
- 5 small garlic cloves, halved
- 4 (4-ounces) (½-inch thick) grass-fed lamb loin chops, trimmed
- 1/8 teaspoon dried thyme, crushed
- 1/8 teaspoon red pepper flakes, crushed
- Salt and ground black pepper, as required
- 1 tablespoon fresh lemon juice
- 1½ tablespoons water
- 1½ tablespoons fresh parsley, finely chopped and divided

Method:

1. In a large skillet, melt the butter over medium-high heat and sauté the garlic for about 1 minute.
2. Add the lamb chops, thyme, red pepper flakes, salt, and black pepper and cook for about 3-4 minutes per side.
3. Divide the chops onto serving plates, leaving the garlic in skillet.
4. In the skillet, add the lemon juice, water and half of the parsley and cook for about 1 minute, stirring continuously.
5. Pour the sauce evenly over the chops.
6. Garnish with the remaining parsley and serve.

Nutritional Value:

- *Calories 513*
- *Total Fat 25.4 g*
- *Saturated Fat 11.5 g*
- *Cholesterol 227 mg*
- *Total Carbs 2.9 g*

- *Sugar 0.3 g*
- *Fiber 0.3 g*
- *Sodium 316 mg*
- *Potassium 821 mg*
- *Protein 64.4 g*

Cheese and Walnut Coated Lamb Chops

Preparation Time: 15 minutes
Cooking Time: 10 minutes
Servings: 2

Ingredients:

- 1 tablespoon butter
- 2 (10½-ounce) grass-fed lamb chops
- ¼ cup Brie cheese
- ¼ tablespoon fresh rosemary, chopped
- 2 tablespoons walnuts, chopped roughly
- Ground black pepper, as required

Method:

1. Preheat the broiler of oven to medium-high heat. Grease a broiler pan.
2. In a large frying pan, melt the butter over medium heat and cook the lamb chops for about 2-3 minutes per side or until browned.
3. Meanwhile, in a bowl, add the remaining ingredients and mix well.
4. Arrange the lamb chops onto the prepared broiler pan and top each with walnut mixture.
5. Broil for about 2-4 minutes or until the cheese is melted.

Nutritional Value:

- Calories 714
- Total Fat 37.2 g
- Saturated Fat 14.9 g
- Cholesterol 301 mg
- Total Carbs 1.1 g
- Sugar 0.2 g
- Fiber 0.7 g
- Sodium 381 mg
- Potassium 1072 mg
- Protein 89.3 g

Braised Lamb Shanks

Preparation Time: 15 minutes
Cooking Time: 2 hours 40 minutes
Servings: 2

Ingredients:

- 2 tablespoons butter
- 2 (12-ounce) grass-fed lamb shanks
- 1 small yellow onion, chopped
- 3 garlic cloves, minced
- 1 teaspoon ground coriander
- 1 teaspoon ground cumin
- ½ teaspoon red chili powder
- ¼ teaspoon ground turmeric
- Salt, as required
- 3 cups homemade chicken broth
- 2 bay leaves

Method:

1. Preheat the oven to 325 degrees F.
2. In an oven proof pan, melt the butter over medium-high heat and cook the lamb shanks for about 3-4 minutes, flipping once halfway through.
3. With a slotted spoon, transfer the shanks onto a plate.
4. In the same pan, add onion, garlic, spices, and salt and sauté for about 40-60 seconds.
5. Add the cooked shanks, broth, and bay leaves and bring to a boil.
6. Immediately, cover the pan and transfer into the oven.
7. Bake for about 2¼ hours, flipping the shanks after every 45 minutes.
8. Remove the lid and bake for about 20 more minutes.
9. Remove the pan from oven and discard the bay leaves.
10. Serve hot.

Nutritional Value:

- *Calories 820*
- *Total Fat 38.9 g*

- Saturated Fat 16.8 g
- Cholesterol 337 mg
- Total Carbs 7.2 g
- Sugar 2.7 g

- Fiber 1.2 g
- Sodium 1500 mg
- Potassium 1561 mg
- Protein 103.9 g

Chapter 10: Poultry Recipes

Parmesan Chicken

Preparation Time: 15 minutes
Cooking Time: 27 minutes
Servings: 2

Ingredients:

- 1 small organic egg, beaten
- ½ tablespoon water
- ¾ cup Parmesan cheese, shredded
- 1/8 teaspoon garlic powder
- Salt and ground black pepper, as required
- 2 (5-ounce) grass-fed boneless, skinless chicken breasts
- ½ cup olive oil
- ¼ cup Asiago cheese, shredded
- 2 cooked bacon slices, crumbled

Method:

1. Preheat the oven to 350 degrees F. Arrange a rack into a foil-lined baking dish.
2. In a small shallow dish, add the egg and water and beat lightly.
3. In another shallow dish, add the Parmesan cheese, garlic powder, salt and black pepper and mix well.
4. Dip each chicken breast in egg mixture evenly and then coat with the cheese mixture.
5. In a deep skillet, heat the oil over medium-high heat and fry chicken breasts for about 3-4 minutes or until golden brown from both sides.
6. With a slotted spoon, transfer the chicken breasts into the prepared baking dish in a single layer.
7. Bake for about 20 minutes or until chicken is cooked through.
8. Now, set the oven to broiler.
9. Remove the baking dish from the oven and sprinkle the chicken breasts with Asiago cheese, followed by the bacon.
10. Broil for about 2-3 minutes or until cheese is melted and bubbly.
11. Serve hot.

Nutritional Value:

- Calories 514
- Total Fat 27.8 g
- Saturated Fat 12.3 g
- Cholesterol 214 mg
- Total Carbs 2 g

- Sugar 0.2 g
- Fiber 0 g
- Sodium 203 mg
- Potassium 1500 mg
- Protein 61.7 g

Baked Chicken Leg Quarters

Preparation Time: 15 minutes
Cooking Time: 63 minutes
Servings: 2

Ingredients:

- 2 (10-ounce) grass-fed bone-in, skin-on chicken leg quarters
- 1/3 cup mayonnaise
- ¾ teaspoon paprika
- ½ teaspoon garlic powder
- Salt and ground white pepper, as required

Method:

1. Preheat the oven to 350 degrees. Generously, grease a baking dish.
2. In a shallow bowl, place the mayonnaise.
3. In a small bowl, add the paprika, garlic powder, salt and white pepper and mix well.
4. Coat each chicken leg quarter with the mayonnaise and then, sprinkle with the spice mixture evenly.
5. Arrange the chicken quarters onto the prepared baking sheet in a single layer.
6. Bake for about 45 minutes.
7. Now, increase the temperature of oven to 400 degrees F and bake for about 5-8 minutes.
8. Remove from the oven and place the chicken quarters onto a platter.
9. With a piece of foil, cover each chicken quarter loosely for about 5-10 minutes before serving.

Nutritional Value:

- Calories 726
- Total Fat 59.7 g
- Saturated Fat 12.9 g
- Cholesterol 228 mg
- Total Carbs 1 g
- Sugar 0.3 g
- Fiber 0.4 g
- Sodium 774 mg
- Potassium 26 mg
- Protein 48.3 g

Stuffed Chicken Breasts

Preparation Time: 15 minutes
Cooking Time: 33 minutes
Servings: 2

Ingredients:

For Chicken Marinade:

- 1½ tablespoons balsamic vinegar
- 1½ tablespoons olive oil
- 1 tablespoon water
- 1 garlic clove, minced
- ½ teaspoon dried Italian seasoning
- ¼ teaspoon dried rosemary
- Salt and ground black pepper, as required
- 2 (6-ounce) grass-fed skinless, boneless chicken breasts

For Stuffing:

- 8 fresh basil leaves
- 1 small fresh tomato, sliced thinly
- 2 provolone cheese slices
- 6 bacon slices
- 2 tablespoons Parmesan cheese, grated freshly

Method:

1. For marinade: In a bowl, add all ingredients except chicken and mix until well combined.
2. Place 1 chicken breasts onto a smooth surface.
3. Hold a sharp knife parallel to work surface, slice the chicken breast horizontally, without cutting all the way through.
4. Repeat with the remaining chicken breasts.
5. Place the breasts in the bowl of marinade and toss to coat well.
6. Refrigerate, covered for at least 30 minutes.
7. Preheat the oven to 500 degrees F. Grease a baking dish.

8. Remove the chicken breasts from bowl and arrange onto a smooth surface.
9. Place 4 basil leaves onto the bottom half of a chicken breast, followed by 2-3 tomato slices and 1 provolone cheese slice.
10. Now, fold the top half over filling.
11. Wrap the breast with 3 bacon slices and secure wit toothpicks.
12. Repeat with the remaining chicken breast and filling.
13. Arrange breasts into the prepared baking dish in a single layer.
14. Bake for about 30 minutes, flipping once in the halfway through.
15. Remove from the oven and sprinkle each chicken breast with the Parmesan cheese evenly.
16. Bake for about 2-3 minutes more.
17. Serve hot.

Nutritional Value:

- *Calories 706*
- *Total Fat 47.6 g*
- *Saturated Fat 14.9 g*
- *Cholesterol 220 mg*
- *Total Carbs 5 g*

- *Sugar 3.5 g*
- *Fiber 0.7 g*
- *Sodium 1700 mg*
- *Potassium 393 mg*
- *Protein 64 g*

Butter Chicken

Preparation Time: 15 minutes
Cooking Time: 25 minutes
Servings: 2

Ingredients:

- 1 tablespoon unsalted butter
- 1 small yellow onion, chopped
- 1 garlic clove, minced
- ½ teaspoon fresh ginger, minced
- ¾ pound grass-fed chicken breasts, cut into ¾-inch chunks
- 2 ounces canned sugar-free tomato paste
- 1 teaspoon garam masala
- ½ teaspoon red chili powder
- ½ teaspoon ground cumin
- Salt and ground black pepper, as required
- ½ cup heavy cream
- 1 tablespoon fresh cilantro, chopped

Method:

1. In a large skillet, melt the butter over medium-high heat and sauté the onions for about 4-5 minutes.
2. Add the garlic and ginger and sauté for about 1 minute.
3. Add the chicken, tomato paste and spices and cook for about 6-8 minutes or until desired doneness of the chicken.
4. Stir in the heavy cream and cook for about 8-10 minutes, stirring occasionally.
5. Serve hot with the garnishing of cilantro.

Nutritional Value:

- *Calories 524*
- *Total Fat 29.7 g*
- *Saturated Fat 14.1 g*
- *Cholesterol 208 mg*
- *Total Carbs 10 g*
- *Sugar 4 g*
- *Fiber 2 g*
- *Sodium 238 mg*
- *Potassium 519 mg*
- *Protein 52.3 g*

Chicken Parmigiana

Preparation Time: 15 minutes
Cooking Time: 26 minutes
Servings: 2

Ingredients:

- 1 small organic egg, beaten
- ¼ cup superfine blanched almond flour
- 2 tablespoons Parmesan cheese, grated
- ¼ teaspoon dried parsley
- ¼ teaspoon paprika
- ¼ teaspoon garlic powder
- Salt and ground black pepper, as required
- 2 (6-ounce) grass-fed skinless, boneless chicken breasts, pounded into ½-inch thickness
- 2 tablespoons olive oil
- 1/3 cup sugar-free marinara sauce
- 2 ounces mozzarella cheese, sliced thinly
- 1 tablespoon fresh parsley, chopped

Method:

1. Preheat the oven to 375 degrees F.
2. In a shallow dish, place the beaten egg.
3. In another shallow dish, place the almond flour, Parmesan, parsley, spices, salt, and black pepper and mix well.
4. Dip each chicken breast into the beaten egg and then, coat with the flour mixture.
5. In a deep skillet, heat the oil over medium-high heat and fry the chicken breasts for about 3 minutes per side.
6. With a slotted spoon, transfer the chicken breasts onto a paper towel-lined plate to drain.
7. In the bottom of a small casserole dish, place about ¼ cup of marinara sauce and spread evenly.
8. Arrange the chicken breasts over marinara sauce in a single layer.
9. Top with the remaining marinara sauce, followed by mozzarella cheese slices.
10. Bake for about 20 minutes or until done completely.

11. Remove from the oven and serve hot with the garnishing of fresh parsley.

Nutritional Value:

- Calories 553
- Total Fat 34.8 g
- Saturated Fat 9 g
- Cholesterol 187 mg
- Total Carbs 6.6 g

- Sugar 1.6 g
- Fiber 2.3 g
- Sodium 506 mg
- Potassium 36 mg
- Protein 54.1 g

Chicken with Cranberries

Preparation Time: 15 minutes
Cooking Time: 25 minutes
Servings: 2

Ingredients:

- 1 tablespoon unsalted butter, divided
- 2 (6-ounce) grass-fed skinless, boneless chicken thighs
- Freshly ground black pepper, as required
- 2 tablespoons onion, chopped finely
- 1 teaspoon fresh ginger, minced
- ½ cup homemade chicken broth
- ½ tablespoon fresh lemon juice
- ½ cup fresh cranberries
- 1 teaspoon Erythritol

Method:

1. In a large skillet, melt 1 tablespoon of the butter over medium heat and cook the chicken with salt and black pepper for about 5-6 minutes per side or until done completely.
2. Transfer the chicken thighs into a large bowl and cover with a piece of foil to keep warm.
3. In the same skillet, add the onion over medium heat and sauté for about 2-3 minutes.
4. Add the chicken broth and bring to a boil, stirring occasionally to loosen the brown bits of skillet.
5. Stir in the cranberries and cook or about 5 minutes.
6. Stir in the Erythritol, salt and black pepper and cook for about 1-2 minutes.
7. Stir in the remaining butter and remove from the heat.
8. Pour the cranberry mixture over the chicken and serve.

Nutritional Value:

- *Calories 296*
- *Total Fat 12.3 g*
- *Saturated Fat 6.1 g*
- *Cholesterol 114 mg*

- Total Carbs 4.4 g
- Sugar 1.7 g
- Fiber 1.4 g

- Sodium 294 mg
- Potassium 132 mg
- Protein 39.5 g

Chicken with Spinach

Preparation Time: 15 minutes
Cooking Time: 15 minutes
Servings: 2

Ingredients:

- 1 tablespoon butter, divided
- ½ pound grass-fed chicken tenders
- Salt and ground black pepper, as required
- 1 garlic clove, minced
- 6 ounces frozen chopped spinach, thawed
- 2 tablespoons Parmesan cheese, shredded
- 2 tablespoons heavy cream

Method:

1. In a large skillet, melt 1 tablespoon of the butter over medium-high heat and cook the chicken with salt and black pepper for about 2-3 minutes per side.
2. Transfer the chicken into a bowl.
3. In the same skillet, melt the remaining butter over medium-low heat and sauté the garlic for about 1 minute.
4. Add the spinach and cook for about 1 minute.
5. Add the cheese, cream, salt and black pepper and stir to combine.
6. Spread the spinach mixture in the bottom of skillet evenly.
7. Place the chicken tenders over the spinach in a single layer.
8. Immediately, reduce the heat to low and simmer, covered for about 5 minutes or until desired doneness of the chicken.
9. Serve hot.

Nutritional Value:

- *Calories 361*
- *Total Fat 21.4 g*
- *Saturated Fat 10.3 g*
- *Cholesterol 140 mg*
- *Total Carbs 4.2 g*
- *Sugar 0.4 g*
- *Fiber 1.9 g*
- *Sodium 374 mg*
- *Potassium 774 mg*
- *Protein 37.6 g*

Chicken in Capers Sauce

Preparation Time: 15 minutes
Cooking Time: 25 minutes
Servings: 2

Ingredients:

- 2 (5½ oz.) grass-fed boneless, skinless chicken thighs, cut in half horizontally
- Salt and ground black pepper, as required
- 1/3 cup almond flour
- 2 tablespoons Parmesan cheese, shredded
- ½ teaspoon garlic powder
- 2 tablespoons butter, divided
- 1 teaspoon garlic, minced
- 3 tablespoons capers
- ¼ teaspoon red pepper flakes, crushed
- 2 tablespoons fresh lemon juice
- 1 cup homemade chicken broth
- 1/3 cup heavy cream
- 2 tablespoons fresh parsley, chopped

Method:

1. Season the chicken thighs with the salt and black pepper evenly.
2. In a shallow dish, add the flour, Parmesan cheese and garlic powder.
3. Coat the chicken thighs with flour mixture and then shake off any excess.
4. In a large skillet, melt 1 tbsp. of the butter over medium-high heat and cook the chicken thighs for about 4-5 minutes per side.
5. With a slotted spoon, place the chicken thighs onto a platter and with a piece of foil, cover them to keep warm.
6. In a bowl, add the capers, garlic, red pepper flakes, lemon juice, and broth and beat until well combined.
7. In the same skillet, melt the remaining butter over medium heat and with a spoon, scrape the brown bits from the bottom.
8. Stir in the capers mixture and cook for about 8-10 minutes or until desired thickness, stirring occasionally.
9. Remove from heat and stir in the heavy cream until smooth.

10. Again, place the skillet over medium heat and cook for about 1 minute.
11. Stir in the cooked chicken and cook for about 1 more minute.
12. Garnish with fresh parsley and serve hot.

Nutritional Value:

- Calories 632
- Total Fat 41.7 g
- Saturated Fat 17 g
- Cholesterol 200 mg
- Total Carbs 7.5 g

- Sugar 1 g
- Fiber 2.8 g
- Sodium 1100 mg
- Potassium 568 mg
- Protein 54.7 g

Bacon Wrapped Turkey Breast

Preparation Time: 15 minutes
Cooking Time: 1 hour
Servings: 2

Ingredients:

- ¾ pound turkey breast
- ½ teaspoon dried thyme
- ½ teaspoon dried rosemary
- ½ teaspoon dried sage
- Salt and ground black pepper, as required
- 6 large bacon slices

Method:

1. Preheat the oven to 350 degrees F. Line a baking sheet with parchment paper.
2. Sprinkle the turkey breast with herb mixture, salt and black pepper.
3. Arrange the bacon slices onto a smooth surface in a row with the slices, pressing against each other.
4. Place the turkey breast on top of the bacon slices.
5. Wrap the end pieces of bacon around the turkey breast first, followed by the middle pieces.
6. Arrange wrapped turkey breast onto the prepared baking sheet.
7. With a piece of foil, cover the turkey breast loosely and bake for about 50 minutes.
8. Remove the foil and bake for about 10 more minutes.
9. Remove from the oven and place the turkey breast onto a platter for about 5-10 minutes before slicing.
10. With a sharp knife, cut the turkey breast into desired size slices and serve.

Nutritional Value:

- Calories 650
- Total Fat 39.3 g
- Saturated Fat 12.6 g
- Cholesterol 169 mg
- Total Carbs 8 g

- Sugar 6 g
- Fiber 1.1 g
- Sodium 381 mg
- Potassium 1012 mg
- Protein 61.3g

Spiced Ground Turkey

Preparation Time: 15 minutes
Cooking Time: 20 minutes
Servings: 2

Ingredients:

For Spices Blend:

- ½ teaspoon xanthan gum
- ½ teaspoon ground cumin
- ½ teaspoon ground coriander
- Pinch of ground cloves
- Pinch of ground cinnamon
- Pinch of ground turmeric
- Pinch of cayenne pepper
- Salt and ground black pepper, as required

For Turkey:

- ¾ pound ground turkey
- ½ of small yellow onion, sliced
- ½ teaspoon fresh ginger, minced
- ½ teaspoon garlic, minced
- 1 small tomato, chopped
- 2-3 tablespoons water
- ¼ cup unsweetened coconut milk
- 1 tablespoon fresh cilantro, chopped
- 1½ tablespoons sour cream

Method:

1. For spice blend: add all ingredients in a bowl and mix well. Set aside.
2. Heat a nonstick skillet over medium-high heat and cook the turkey, onion, ginger and garlic for about 5-6 minutes or until browned completely.
3. With a slotted spoon, discard any excess fat from the skillet.
4. Stir in the spice blend and cook for about 2 minutes, stirring frequently.

5. Stir in the remaining ingredients except cilantro and bring to a gentle boil.
6. Reduce the heat to medium-low and cook for about 10 minutes.
7. Stir in the cilantro and remove from the heat.
8. Serve immediately with the topping of sour cream.

Nutritional Value:

- Calories 385
- Total Fat 21.4 g
- Saturated Fat 4.8 g
- Cholesterol 177 mg
- Total Carbs 6.8 g
- Sugar 2 g
- Fiber 3 g
- Sodium 304 mg
- Potassium 637 mg
- Protein 47.6 g

Chapter 11: Seafood Recipes

Roasted Trout

Preparation Time: 15 minutes
Cooking Time: 25 minutes
Servings: 2

Ingredients:

- 1 (1½-pound) wild-caught trout, gutted and cleaned
- Salt and ground black pepper, as required
- ½ lemon, sliced
- 1 tablespoon fresh dill, minced
- 1 tablespoon butter, melted
- 1 tablespoon fresh lemon juice

Method:

1. Preheat the oven to 475 degrees F. Arrange a wire rack onto a foil-lined baking sheet.
2. Sprinkle the trout with salt and pepper from inside and outside generously.
3. Fill the fish cavity with lemon slices and dill
4. Place the trout onto the prepared baking sheet and drizzle with the melted butter and lemon juice.
5. Bake for about 25 minutes.
6. Serve hot.

Nutritional Value:

- *Calories 589*
- *Total Fat 32.6 g*
- *Saturated Fat 10.3 g*
- *Cholesterol 146 mg*
- *Total Carbs 1 g*
- *Sugar 0.2 g*
- *Fiber 0.2 g*
- *Sodium 896 mg*
- *Potassium 1300 mg*
- *Protein 73.3 g*

Cod in Butter Sauce

Preparation Time: 15 minutes
Cooking Time: 10 minutes
Servings: 2

Ingredients:

- 2 (6-ounces) cod fillets
- 1 teaspoon onion powder
- Salt and ground black pepper, as required
- 3 tablespoons butter, divided
- 2 garlic cloves, minced
- 1-2 lemon slices
- 2 teaspoons fresh dill weed

Method:

1. Season each cod fillet evenly with the onion powder, salt and black pepper.
2. Melt 1 tablespoon of butter in a medium skillet over high heat and cook the cod fillets for about 4-5 minutes per side.
3. Transfer the cod fillets onto a plate.
4. Meanwhile, in a frying pan, melt the remaining butter over low heat and sauté the garlic and lemon slices for about 40-60 seconds.
5. Stir in the cooked cod fillets and dill and cook, covered for about 1-2 minutes.
6. Remove the cod fillets from heat and transfer onto the serving plates.
7. Top with the pan sauce and serve immediately.

Nutritional Value:

- Calories 302
- Total Fat 18.9 g
- Saturated Fat 10.9g
- Cholesterol 129 mg
- Total Carbs 2.9 g
- Sugar 0.6 g
- Fiber 0.4 g
- Sodium 310 mg
- Potassium 66 mg
- Protein 31.1 g

Stuffed Salmon

Preparation Time: 15 minutes
Cooking Time: 16 minutes
Servings: 2

Ingredients:

For Salmon:

- 2 (6-ounce) skinless salmon fillets
- Salt and ground black pepper, as required
- 1 tablespoon fresh lemon juice
- 1 tablespoon olive oil, divided
- 1 tablespoon unsalted butter

For Filling:

- 2 ounces cream cheese, softened
- 2 tablespoons Parmesan cheese, grated finely
- 2 ounces frozen spinach, thawed and squeezed
- 1 teaspoon garlic, minced
- Salt and ground black pepper, as required

Method:

1. Season each salmon fillet with salt and black pepper and then, drizzle with the lemon juice and ½ tablespoon of the oil evenly.
2. Arrange the salmon fillets onto a smooth surface.
3. With a sharp knife, cut a pocket into each salmon fillet about ¾ of the way through, being careful not to cut all the way.
4. For filling: in a bowl, place the cream cheese, Parmesan cheese, spinach, garlic, salt and black pepper and mix well.
5. Place about 1-2 tablespoons of the spinach mixture into each salmon pocket and spread evenly.
6. Heat the remaining oil and butter and in a skillet over medium-high heat and cook the salmon fillets for about 6-8 minutes per side.
7. Remove the salmon fillets from the heat and transfer onto the serving plates.

8. Serve immediately.

Nutritional Value:

- Calories 463
- Total Fat 34.5 g
- Saturated Fat 13.1 g
- Cholesterol 125 mg
- Total Carbs 2.4 g

- Sugar 0.4 g
- Fiber 0.7 g
- Sodium 341 mg
- Potassium 862 mg
- Protein 38.2 g

Salmon with Cream Cheese

Preparation Time: 15 minutes
Cooking Time: 20 minutes
Servings: 2

Ingredients:

- ¼ cup cream cheese, softened
- 2 tablespoons fresh chives, chopped
- ½ teaspoon garlic powder
- ¼ teaspoon cayenne pepper
- Salt and ground black pepper, as required
- 2 (5-ounces) salmon fillets

Method:

1. Preheat the oven to 350 degrees F and lightly, grease a small baking dish.
2. Add the cream cheese, chives, spices, salt and black pepper in a bowl and mix well.
3. Arrange the salmon fillets into the prepared baking dish and top evenly with the cream cheese mixture.
4. Bake for about 15-20 minutes or until desired doneness of the salmon.
5. Remove the salmon fillets from oven and transfer onto the serving plates.
6. Serve hot.

Nutritional Value:

- Calories 293
- Total Fat 18.9 g
- Saturated Fat 7.6 g
- Cholesterol 94 mg
- Total Carbs 1.5 g
- Sugar 0.3 g
- Fiber 0.2 g
- Sodium 226 mg
- Potassium 600 mg
- Protein 29.9 g

Parmesan Halibut

Preparation Time: 15 minutes
Cooking Time: 24 minutes
Servings: 2

Ingredients:

- 2 (6-ounces) halibut fillets
- Salt and ground black pepper, as required
- 3 tablespoons sour cream
- ¼ teaspoon dill weed
- ¼ teaspoon garlic powder
- 2 tablespoons Parmesan cheese, grated
- 3 tablespoons scallions, chopped and divided

Method:

1. Preheat the oven to 375 degrees F and line a medium baking sheet with parchment paper.
2. Season each halibut fillet with salt and black pepper.
3. Add the sour cream, dill weed, and garlic powder in a bowl and mix until well combined.
4. Stir in the Parmesan cheese and 2 tablespoons of scallion.
5. Arrange the halibut fillets onto prepared baking sheet and top each evenly with Parmesan mixture.
6. Bake for about 24 minutes or until desired doneness.
7. Remove the halibut fillets from oven and transfer onto the serving plates.
8. Top with the remaining scallions and serve immediately.

Nutritional Value:

- Calories 292
- Total Fat 11.8 g
- Saturated Fat 5.4 g
- Cholesterol 78 mg
- Total Carbs 2.8 g
- Sugar 0.3 g
- Fiber 0.3 g
- Sodium 558 mg
- Potassium 331 mg
- Protein 42.6 g

Prawns in Mushroom Sauce

Preparation Time: 15 minutes
Cooking Time: 15 minutes
Servings: 2

Ingredients:

- 4 bacon slices, cut into 1-inch pieces
- 1¼ cups fresh mushrooms, sliced
- 8 ounces prawns, peeled and deveined
- 1½ cups heavy whipping cream
- 1 jalapeño pepper, chopped
- 1 teaspoon fresh thyme, chopped
- Salt and ground black pepper, as required

Method:

1. Heat a skillet over medium heat and cook the bacon for about 5 minutes, stirring frequently.
2. Add the mushrooms and cook for about 5-6 minutes, stirring frequently.
3. Add the prawns and stir to combine.
4. Increase the heat to high and stir fry for about 2 minutes
5. Add the cream, jalapeño pepper, thyme, salt, and black pepper and stir to combine.
6. Reduce the heat to medium and cook for about 1 more minute.
7. Remove the skillet from heat and serve hot.

Nutritional Value:

- Calories 772
- Total Fat 59.7 g
- Saturated Fat 29.3 g
- Cholesterol 426 mg
- Total Carbs 7.2 g
- Sugar 1.1 g
- Fiber 0.8 g
- Sodium 1700 mg
- Potassium 746 mg
- Protein 50.7 g

Shrimp with Zucchini Pasta

Preparation Time: 15 minutes
Cooking Time: 7 minutes
Servings: 2

Ingredients:

- 1 tablespoon unsalted butter
- 1 small garlic clove, minced
- 1/8 teaspoon red pepper flakes, crushed
- ½ pound medium shrimp, peeled and deveined
- Salt and ground black pepper, as required
- 3-4 tablespoons homemade chicken broth
- 1 medium zucchini, spiralized with blade C
- 1 tablespoon fresh parsley, chopped finely

Method:

1. Heat the oil in a large skillet over medium heat and sauté garlic and red pepper flakes for about 1 minute.
2. Add shrimp and black pepper and cook for about 1 minute per side.
3. Add broth and zucchini noodles and cook for about 3-4 minutes.
4. Garnish with parsley and serve hot.

Nutritional Value:

- Calories 208
- Total Fat 8 g
- Saturated Fat 4.3 g
- Cholesterol 254 mg
- Total Carbs 5.8 g
- Sugar 1.8 g
- Fiber 1.2 g
- Sodium 678 mg
- Potassium 489 mg
- Protein 27.7 g

Buttered Scallops

Preparation Time: 15 minutes
Cooking Time: 5 minutes
Servings: 2

Ingredients:

- 2 tablespoons unsalted butter
- 2 tablespoons fresh rosemary, chopped
- 1 garlic clove, minced
- ¾ pound sea scallops

Method:

1. In a medium skillet, melt the butter over medium-high heat and sauté the rosemary and garlic for about 1 minute.
2. Add the scallops and cook for about 2 minutes per side or until desired doneness.
3. Remove from the heat and serve hot.

Nutritional Value:

- *Calories 265*
- *Total Fat 13.3 g*
- *Saturated Fat 7.7 g*
- *Cholesterol 87 mg*
- *Total Carbs 6.6 g*
- *Sugar 0 g*
- *Fiber 1.4 g*
- *Sodium 358 mg*
- *Potassium 589 mg*
- *Protein 28.9 g*

Scallops with Broccoli

Preparation Time: 15 minutes
Cooking Time: 5 minutes
Servings: 2

Ingredients:

For Broccoli:

- ½ pounds small broccoli florets
- 1 tablespoon unsalted butter, melted

For Scallops:

- 1 tablespoon butter
- 2 garlic cloves, minced
- ½ pound fresh jumbo scallops, rinsed and pat dried
- Salt and ground black pepper, as required
- 1 tablespoon fresh lemon juice
- 1 scallion (green part), sliced thinly

Method:

1. For broccoli: arrange a steamer basket in a pan of water and bring to a boil.
2. Place broccoli in steamer basket and steam, covered for about 4-5 minutes.
3. Meanwhile, in a large skillet, melt the butter over medium-high heat and sauté the garlic for about 1 minute.
4. Add the scallops and cook for about 2 minutes per side.
5. Stir in the salt, black pepper and lemon juice and remove from heat.
6. Drain broccoli and drizzle with oil evenly.
7. Divide the cooked broccoli onto serving plates and top with scallops evenly.
8. Serve immediately with the garnishing of scallion.

Nutritional Value:

- *Calories 247*
- *Total Fat 12.3 g*
- *Saturated Fat 8.2 g*
- *Cholesterol 67 mg*

- *Total Carbs 11 g*
- *Sugar 2.3 g*
- *Fiber 3.2 g*

- *Sodium 301 mg*
- *Potassium 766 mg*
- *Protein 22.6 g*

Lemony Crab Legs

Preparation Time: 15 minutes
Cooking Time: 5 minutes
Servings: 2

Ingredients:

- 1-pound king crab legs
- 4 tablespoons unsalted butter, melted
- 1 tablespoon fresh parsley, chopped
- 3 garlic cloves, minced
- 1 tablespoon fresh lemon juice

Method:

1. Preheat the oven to 375 degrees F.
2. With a sharp knife, cut the crab legs into halves to expose the flesh.
3. Add the butter, parsley, garlic and ½ tablespoon of lemon juice in a bowl and mix well.
4. In a small bowl, reserve about ¼ of the butter mixture.
5. Arrange the crab legs onto a baking sheet and drizzle with the remaining butter mixture.
6. Bake for about 5 minutes.
7. Remove the crab legs from oven and transfer onto the serving plates.
8. Drizzle with the reserved butter mixture and remaining lemon juice and serve immediately.

Nutritional Value:

- Calories 442
- Total Fat 26.6 g
- Saturated Fat 14.7 g
- Cholesterol 187 mg
- Total Carbs 1.8 g
- Sugar 0.3 g
- Fiber 0.2 g
- Sodium 2500 mg
- Potassium 45 mg
- Protein 44.2 g

Chapter 12: Soups & Sides Recipes

Asparagus Soup

Preparation Time: 15 minutes
Cooking Time: 35 minutes
Servings: 2

Ingredients:

- 1 tablespoon olive oil
- 2 scallions, chopped
- ¾ pound fresh asparagus, trimmed and chopped
- 2 cups homemade vegetable broth
- 1 tablespoon fresh lemon juice
- Salt and ground black pepper, as required
- 1 tablespoons cream

Method:

1. In a large pan, heat the oil over medium heat and sauté the scallion for about 4-5 minutes.
2. Stir in the asparagus and broth and bring to a boil.
3. Reduce the heat to low and simmer, covered for about 20-25 minutes.
4. Remove from the heat and set aside to cool slightly.
5. Now, transfer the soup into a high-speed blender in 2 batches and pulse until smooth.
6. Return the soup into the same pan over medium heat and simmer for about 4-5 minutes.
7. Stir in the lemon juice, salt and black pepper and remove from the heat.
8. Serve hot with the topping of the cream.

Nutritional Value:

- Calories 143
- Total Fat 9 g
- Saturated Fat 1.7 g
- Cholesterol 1 mg
- Total Carbs 9 g
- Sugar 4.5 g
- Fiber 4 g
- Sodium 850 mg
- Potassium 603 mg
- Protein 9 g

Broccoli Soup

Preparation Time: 15 minutes
Cooking Time: 15 minutes
Servings: 2

Ingredients:

- 2 cups homemade chicken broth
- 10 ounces small broccoli florets
- 6 ounces cheddar cheese, cubed
- Freshly ground black pepper, as required
- ½ cup heavy cream

Method:

1. In a large soup pan, add the broth and broccoli over medium-high heat and bring to a boil.
2. Reduce the heat to low and simmer, covered for about 5-7 minutes.
3. Stir in the cheese and simmer for about 2-3 minutes, stirring continuously until cheese is melted completely.
4. Stir in the black pepper and cream and simmer for about 2 minutes.
5. Serve hot.

Nutritional Value:

- Calories 521
- Total Fat 40.7 g
- Saturated Fat 25.2 g
- Cholesterol 130 mg
- Total Carbs 10 g
- Sugar 3 g
- Fiber 3.6 g
- Sodium 1330 mg
- Potassium 731 mg
- Protein 30.3 g

Chicken Soup

Preparation Time: 15 minutes
Cooking Time: 4 minutes
Servings: 2

Ingredients:

- 2 tablespoons unsalted butter
- 2 medium jalapeño peppers, seeded and chopped
- ½ small yellow onion, chopped
- ½ teaspoon dried thyme, crushed
- ¼ teaspoon ground cumin
- 1½ cups homemade chicken broth
- 3 ounces cheddar cheese, shredded
- 1/3 cup heavy cream
- Salt and ground black pepper, as required
- 2 cooked bacon slices, chopped

Method:

1. In a large pan, melt ½ tablespoon of the butter over medium heat and sauté the jalapeño peppers for about 1-2 minutes.
2. With a slotted spoon, transfer the jalapeño peppers onto a plate.
3. In the same pan, melt the remaining butter over medium heat and sauté the onion for about 3-4 minutes.
4. Add the spices and sauté for about 1 minute.
5. Add the broth and bring to a boil.
6. Reduce the heat to low and cook for about 10 minutes.
7. Remove from the heat and with an immersion blender, blend until smooth.
8. Return the pan over medium-low heat.
9. Stir in 1 bacon slice, cooked jalapeño, cheese, cream and black pepper and cook for about 5 minutes.
10. Serve hot with the topping of remaining bacon.

Nutritional Value:

- *Calories 542*
- *Total Fat 46.5 g*

- *Saturated Fat 25.2 g*
- *Cholesterol 134 mg*
- *Total Carbs 5.2 g*
- *Sugar 2 g*

- *Fiber 1.1 g*
- *Sodium 2000 mg*
- *Potassium 453 mg*
- *Protein 26 g*

Ground Beef Soup

Preparation Time: 15 minutes
Cooking Time: 30 minutes
Servings: 2

Ingredients:

- ½ pound grass-fed ground beef
- ¼ pound fresh mushrooms, sliced
- ½ small onion, chopped
- 1 garlic clove, minced
- ½ pound head bok choy, stalks and leaves separated and chopped
- 2 cups homemade chicken broth
- Salt and ground black pepper, as required

Method:

1. Heat a large nonstick soup pan over medium-high heat and cook beef for about 5 minutes.
2. Add the onion, mushrooms and garlic and cook for about 5 minutes.
3. Add the bok choy stalks and cook for about 4-5 minutes.
4. Add the broth and bring to a boil.
5. Reduce the heat to low and simmer, covered for about 10 minutes.
6. Stir in the bok choy leaves and simmer for about 5 minutes.
7. Stir in the salt and black pepper and remove from heat.
8. Serve hot with the topping of sour cream.

Nutritional Value:

- *Calories 284*
- *Total Fat 8.9 g*
- *Saturated Fat 3.1 g*
- *Cholesterol 101 mg*
- *Total Carbs 7.3 g*
- *Sugar 3 g*
- *Fiber 2.1 g*
- *Sodium 1160 mg*
- *Potassium 331 mg*
- *Protein 42.9 g*

Salmon Soup

Preparation Time: 15 minutes
Cooking Time: 25 minutes
Servings: 2

Ingredients:

- 1 tablespoon olive oil
- 1 small yellow onion, chopped
- 1 garlic clove, minced
- 2 cups homemade chicken broth
- ½ pound boneless salmon, cubed
- ½ tablespoon low-sodium soy sauce
- 1 tablespoon fresh cilantro, chopped
- Freshly ground black pepper, as required
- ½ tablespoon fresh lime juice

Method:

1. In a large pan heat the oil over medium heat and sauté the onion for about 5 minutes.
2. Add the garlic and sauté for about 1 minute.
3. Stir in the broth and bring to a boil over high heat.
4. Reduce the heat to low and simmer for about 10 minutes.
5. Add the salmon, and soy sauce and cook for about 3-4 minutes.
6. Stir in black pepper, lime juice, and cilantro and remove from the heat.
7. Serve hot.

Nutritional Value:

- Calories 266
- Total Fat 15.4 g
- Saturated Fat 2.4 g
- Cholesterol 50 mg
- Total Carbs 5 g
- Sugar 2.5 g
- Fiber 0.8 g
- Sodium 1035 mg
- Potassium 702 mg
- Protein 27.6 g

Cheesy Spinach

Preparation Time: 15 minutes
Cooking Time: 15 minutes
Servings: 2

Ingredients:

- 1 tablespoon unsalted butter
- 1 small yellow onion, chopped
- ½ cup cream cheese, softened
- 1 (10-ounce) package frozen spinach, thawed and squeezed dry
- 2 tablespoons water
- Salt and ground black pepper, as required
- 1 teaspoon fresh lemon juice

Method:

1. In a skillet, melt the butter over medium heat and sauté the onion for about 6-8 minutes.
2. Add the cream cheese and cook for about 2 minutes till melted completely.
3. Stir in the spinach and water and cook for about 4-5 minutes.
4. Stir in the salt, black pepper and lemon juice and remove from the heat.
5. Serve immediately.

Nutritional Value:

- Calories 301
- Total Fat 26.6 g
- Saturated Fat 16.5 g
- Cholesterol 79 mg
- Total Carbs 10 g
- Sugar 2.3 g
- Fiber 3.9 g
- Sodium 404 mg
- Potassium 916 mg
- Protein 8.9 g

Creamy Brussels Sprout

Preparation Time: 15 minutes
Cooking Time: 15 minutes
Servings: 2

Ingredients:

- ¾ pound fresh Brussels sprouts, trimmed and halved
- 1 garlic clove, minced
- 1 tablespoon butter, melted
- 1 tablespoon Dijon mustard
- ¼ cup heavy whipping cream
- Salt and ground white pepper, as required

Method:

1. Preheat the oven to 450 degrees F.
2. In a roasting pan, add the Brussels sprouts, garlic and butter and toss to coat well.
3. Roast for about 10-15 minutes, tossing occasionally.
4. Meanwhile, in a small pan, add the remaining ingredients over medium-low heat and bring to a gentle boil.
5. Cook for about 1-2 minutes, stirring continuously.
6. Serve Brussels sprouts with the topping of creamy sauce.

Nutritional Value:

- Calories 125
- Total Fat 11.8 g
- Saturated Fat 7.1 g
- Cholesterol 36 mg
- Total Carbs 3.6 g
- Sugar 0.9 g
- Fiber 1.4 g
- Sodium 222 mg
- Potassium 30 mg
- Protein 1.6 g

Broccoli Stir Fry

Preparation Time: 10 minutes
Cooking Time: 15 minutes
Servings: 2

Ingredients:

- 1 tablespoon coconut oil
- 2 cups broccoli florets
- 1 tablespoon low-sodium soy sauce
- ¼ teaspoon garlic powder
- Ground black pepper, as required

Method:

1. In a large pan, melt the coconut oil over medium heat and stir in the broccoli.
2. Cover the pan and cook for 10 minutes, stirring occasionally.
3. Stir in the soy sauce and spices and cook for about 5 minutes.
4. Serve hot.

Nutritional Value:

- *Calories 93*
- *Total Fat 7.1 g*
- *Saturated Fat 5.9 g*
- *Cholesterol 0 mg*
- *Total Carbs 6.8 g*
- *Sugar 2.1 g*
- *Fiber 2.4 g*
- *Sodium 470 mg*
- *Potassium 292 mg*
- *Protein 3.1 g*

Spicy Mushrooms

Preparation Time: 15 minutes
Cooking Time: 15 minutes
Servings: 2

Ingredients:

- 2 tablespoons butter
- ½ teaspoon cumin seeds, lightly crushed
- 1 small yellow onion, sliced thinly
- ½ pound white button mushrooms, chopped
- 1 jalapeño pepper, chopped
- ½ teaspoon garam masala powder
- 1/3 teaspoon ground coriander
- ½ teaspoon red chili powder
- 1/8 teaspoon ground turmeric
- Salt, as required
- 2 tablespoons fresh cilantro leaves, chopped

Method:

1. In a skillet, melt the butter in a skillet over medium heat and sauté the cumin seeds for about 1 minute.
2. Add the onion and sauté for about 4-5 minutes
3. Add the mushrooms and sauté for about 5-7 minutes.
4. Add the green chili, spices, and salt and sauté for about 1-2 minutes.
5. Stir in the cilantro and sauté for about 1 more minute.
6. Serve hot.

Nutritional Value:

- Calories 147
- Total Fat 12.2 g
- Saturated Fat 7.3 g
- Cholesterol 31 mg
- Total Carbs 8.1 g
- Sugar 3.7 g
- Fiber 2.4 g
- Sodium 176 mg
- Potassium 331 mg
- Protein 4.4 g

Cauliflower Mash

Preparation Time: 15 minutes
Cooking Time: 12 minutes
Servings: 2

Ingredients:

- ½ large head cauliflower, cut into florets
- 3 tablespoons heavy whipping cream
- ½ cup Parmesan cheese, shredded and divided
- ½ tablespoon butter
- Freshly ground black pepper, as required
- ½ tablespoon fresh parsley, chopped

Method:

1. In a large pan of the boiling water, add the cauliflower and cook, covered for about 10-12 minutes.
2. Remove from the heat and drain the cauliflower well.
3. Place the cauliflower, cream, ½ cup of cheese, butter and black pepper in a large food processor and pulse until smooth.
4. Transfer the cauliflower mash into a bowl.
5. Top with the remaining cheese, and parsley and serve.

Nutritional Value:

- Calories 237
- Total Fat 16.9 g
- Saturated Fat 10.5 g
- Cholesterol 53 mg
- Total Carbs 10 g
- Sugar 4 g
- Fiber 5 g
- Sodium 429 mg
- Potassium 649 mg
- Protein 12.1 g

Chapter 13: Desserts Recipes

Mocha Ice Cream

Preparation Time: 15 minutes
Servings: 2

Ingredients:

- 1 cup unsweetened coconut milk
- ¼ cup heavy cream
- 2 tablespoons Erythritol
- 15 drops liquid stevia
- 2 tablespoons cacao powder
- 1 tablespoon instant coffee
- ¼ teaspoon xanthan gum

Method:

1. In a container, add all the ingredients except xanthan gum and with an immersion blender, blend until well combined.
2. Slowly, add the xanthan gum and blend until a slightly thicker mixture is formed.
3. Transfer the mixture into ice cream maker and process according to manufacturer's instructions.
4. Now, transfer the ice cream into an airtight container and freeze for at least 4-5 hours before serving.

Nutritional Value:

- Calories 94
- Total Fat 8.6 g
- Saturated Fat 6.1 g
- Cholesterol 21 mg
- Total Carbs 5.6 g
- Sugar 0 g
- Fiber 3.7 g
- Sodium 41 mg
- Potassium 35 mg
- Protein 1.3 g

Chilled Lemony Treat

Preparation Time: 10 minutes
Servings: 2

Ingredients:

- 2 tablespoons fresh lemon juice
- 4 ounces cream cheese, softened
- ½ cup heavy cream
- Pinch of salt
- ½ teaspoon lemon liquid stevia

Method:

1. In a blender, add the lemon juice and cream cheese and pulse till smooth.
2. Add the remaining ingredients and pulse until well combined and fluffy.
3. Transfer the mixture into serving glasses and refrigerate to chill before serving.

Nutritional Value:

- Calories 305
- Total Fat 31 g
- Saturated Fat 19.5 g
- Cholesterol 103 mg
- Total Carbs 2.7 g
- Sugar 0.5 g
- Fiber 0.1 g
- Sodium 260 mg
- Potassium 109 mg
- Protein 5 g

Spinach Sorbet

Preparation Time: 15 minutes
Servings: 2

Ingredients:

- 1½ cups fresh spinach, chopped
- ½ tablespoon fresh basil leaves
- ¼ of avocado, peeled, pitted and chopped
- 1/3 cup unsweetened almond milk
- 10-12 drops liquid stevia
- ½ teaspoon almonds, chopped very finely
- ½ teaspoon organic vanilla extract
- ½ cup ice cubes

Method:

1. In a blender, add all the ingredients and pulse until creamy and smooth.
2. Transfer into an ice cream maker and process according to manufacturer's directions.
3. Transfer into an airtight container and freeze for at least 4-5 hours.

Nutritional Value:

- Calories 69
- Total Fat 5.8 g
- Saturated Fat 1.1 g
- Cholesterol 0 mg
- Total Carbs 3.6 g
- Sugar 0.4 g
- Fiber 2.4 g
- Sodium 49 mg
- Potassium 286 mg
- Protein 7.9 g

Avocado Mousse

Preparation Time: 15 minutes
Servings: 2

Ingredients:

- 1 ripe avocado, peeled, pitted and chopped
- ¼ cup heavy whipping cream
- ½ teaspoon liquid stevia
- ¼ teaspoon organic vanilla extract
- ¼ teaspoon ground cinnamon

Method:

1. In a bowl, add the avocado and with a potato masher, mash completely.
2. Add the remaining ingredients and mix until well combined.
3. Refrigerate for at least 1 hour before serving.

Nutritional Value:

- *Calories 259*
- *Total Fat 25.2 g*
- *Saturated Fat 7.6 g*
- *Cholesterol 21 mg*
- *Total Carbs 9 g*
- *Sugar 0.6 g*
- *Fiber 6.9 g*
- *Sodium 12 mg*
- *Potassium 331 mg*
- *Protein 2.2 g*

Ricotta Mousse

Preparation Time: 15 minutes
Servings: 2

Ingredients:

- 2½ cups water, divided
- 1 cup ricotta cheese
- 2 teaspoons stevia powder
- 2 teaspoons cacao powder
- ½ teaspoon organic vanilla extract
- 2 tablespoons fresh blackberries

Method:

1. In a large bowl, add all the ingredients except blackberries and beat until well combined.
2. Transfer the mousse into 2 serving glasses and refrigerate to chill for about 4-6 hours or until set completely.
3. Serve with the garnishing of blackberries.

Nutritional Value:

- *Calories 182*
- *Total Fat 10.2 g*
- *Saturated Fat 6.3 g*
- *Cholesterol 38 mg*
- *Total Carbs 8.2 g*
- *Sugar 1 g*
- *Fiber 1 g*
- *Sodium 155 mg*
- *Potassium 331 mg*
- *Protein 14.6 g*

Chocolate Pudding

Preparation Time: 15 minutes
Cooking Time: 4 minutes
Servings: 2

Ingredients:

- 3 tablespoons Erythritol
- 1/8 teaspoon stevia powder
- 2 tablespoons cacao powder
- 1 cup unsweetened coconut milk
- 2 tablespoons heavy cream
- ¼ teaspoon xanthan gum
- 1 tablespoon butter
- ½ teaspoon organic vanilla extract

Method:

1. In a pan, add the Erythritol, stevia powder and cacao powder and mix well.
2. Slowly, add the coconut milk and heavy cream, stirring continuously until well combined.
3. Place the pan over medium heat and bring to a boil, stirring continuously.
4. Cook for about 1 minute, stirring continuously.
5. Remove from the heat and stir in the xanthan gum until well combined.
6. Add the butter and vanilla extract and mix until well combined.
7. Transfer the mixture into a medium bowl.
8. With a plastic wrap, cover the surface of the pudding and refrigerate to chill before serving.
9. Remove from the refrigerator and with an electric mixer, beat the pudding until smooth.
10. Serve immediately.

Nutritional Value:

- *Calories 147*
- *Total Fat 14.3 g*
- *Saturated Fat 9.7 g*
- *Cholesterol 36 mg*
- *Total Carbs 5.7 g*
- *Sugar 0.2 g*

- *Fiber 3.7 g*
- *Sodium 82 mg*
- *Potassium 35 mg*
- *Protein 1.4 g*

Pumpkin Custard

Preparation Time: 10 minutes
Cooking Time: 3 minutes
Servings: 2

Ingredients:

- 1 cup homemade pumpkin puree
- 2 organic eggs
- ½ teaspoon organic vanilla extract
- ¼ teaspoon pumpkin pie spice
- 2 packets stevia
- 2 teaspoons whipped cream

Method:

1. In a small bowl, add all the ingredients and mix until well combined.
2. Transfer the mixture into 2 lightly greased small mugs and microwave for about 2½-3 minutes or until firm.
3. Serve warm with the topping of whipped cream.

Nutritional Value:

- Calories 123
- Total Fat 6.3 g
- Saturated Fat 2.5 g
- Cholesterol 169 mg
- Total Carbs 10 g
- Sugar 4 g
- Fiber 3.6 g
- Sodium 70 mg
- Potassium 319 mg
- Protein 7 g

Vanilla Crème Brûlée

Preparation Time: 15 minutes
Cooking Time: 25 minutes
Servings: 2

Ingredients:

- 1 cup heavy cream
- ½ vanilla bean, halved and scraped out seeds
- 2 organic egg yolks
- ½ teaspoon stevia powder
- ½ teaspoon organic vanilla extract
- Pinch of salt
- 2 tablespoons granulated Erythritol

Method:

1. Preheat the oven to 350 degrees F.
2. In a small pan, add the heavy cream over medium heat and cook until heated.
3. Stir in the vanilla bean seeds and bring to a gentle boil.
4. Reduce the heat to very-low and cook, covered for about 20 minutes.
5. Meanwhile, in a bowl, add the remaining ingredients except Erythritol and beat until thick and pale mixture forms.
6. Remove the heavy cream from heat and through a fine mesh strainer, strain into a heatproof bowl.
7. Slowly, add the cream in egg yolk mixture beating continuously until well combined.
8. Divide the mixture into 2 ramekins evenly.
9. Arrange the ramekins into a large baking dish.
10. In the baking dish, add hot water about half way of the ramekins.
11. Bake for about 30-35 minutes.
12. Remove from the oven and let it cool slightly.
13. Refrigerate the ramekins for at least 4 hours.
14. Just before serving, sprinkle the ramekins with Erythritol evenly.
15. Holding a kitchen torch about 4-5-inch from top, caramelize the Erythritol for about 2 minutes.
16. Set aside for 5 minutes before serving.

Nutritional Value:

- Calories 264
- Total Fat 26.7 g
- Saturated Fat 15.4 g
- Cholesterol 292 mg
- Total Carbs 2.4 g

- Sugar 0.3 g
- Fiber 0 g
- Sodium 109 mg
- Potassium 65 mg
- Protein 3.9 g

Lemon Soufflé

Preparation Time: 15 minutes
Cooking Time: 20 minutes
Servings: 2

Ingredients:

- 1 large organic egg (white and yolk separated)
- 2 tablespoons Erythritol, divided
- ½ cup ricotta cheese
- ½ tablespoon fresh lemon juice
- 1 teaspoon lemon zest, grated
- ½ teaspoon poppy seeds
- ½ teaspoon organic vanilla extract

Method:

1. Preheat the oven to 375 degrees F. Grease 2 ramekins.
2. In a clean glass bowl, add the egg white and beat until foamy.
3. Add 1 tablespoon of the Erythritol and beat until stiff peaks form.
4. In another bowl, add the ricotta cheese, egg yolk and remaining Erythritol and beat until well combined.
5. Now, place the lemon juice and lemon zest and mix well.
6. Add the poppy seeds and vanilla extract and mix until well combined.
7. Add the whipped egg whites into the ricotta mixture and gently, stir to combine.
8. Place the mixture into prepared ramekins evenly.
9. Bake for about 20 minutes.
10. Remove from oven and serve immediately.

Nutritional Value:

- Calories 130
- Total Fat 7.7 g
- Saturated Fat 3.9 g
- Cholesterol 112 mg
- Total Carbs 4 g
- Sugar 0.8 g
- Fiber 0.2 g
- Sodium 114 mg
- Potassium 125 mg
- Protein 10.4 g

Chocolate Lava Cake

Preparation Time: 15 minutes
Cooking Time: 9 minutes
Servings: 2

Ingredients:

- 2 ounces 70% dark chocolate
- 2 ounces unsalted butter
- 2 organic eggs
- 2 tablespoons powdered Erythritol plus more for dusting
- 1 tablespoon almond flour
- 6 fresh raspberries

Method:

1. Preheat the oven to 3500 degrees F. Grease 2 ramekins.
2. In a microwave-safe bowl, add the chocolate and butter and microwave on High for about 2 minutes or until melted, stirring after every 30 seconds.
3. Remove from the microwave and stir until smooth.
4. Place the eggs in a bowl and with a wire whisk, beat well.
5. Add the chocolate mixture, Erythritol and almond flour and mix until well combined.
6. Divide the mixture into the prepared ramekins evenly.
7. Bake for about 9 minutes or until the top is set.
8. Remove from oven and set aside for about 1-2 minutes.
9. Carefully, invert the cakes onto the serving plates and dust with extra powdered Erythritol.
10. Serve with a garnishing of the strawberries.

Nutritional Value:

- *Calories 329*
- *Total Fat 29.9 g*
- *Saturated Fat 16.1 g*
- *Cholesterol 225 mg*
- *Total Carbs 8 g*
- *Sugar 3 g*
- *Fiber 4.7 g*
- *Sodium 230 mg*
- *Potassium 196 mg*
- *Protein 8.3 g*

Conclusion

Several dietary approaches today exist in the world. Every diet promises a different taste and a set of new health benefits. In today's ever-challenging lifestyle, we all need a single formula plan to get all the health benefits at a time. In this context, the Ketogenic diet plan offers a tempting solution. The diet has been in use for several decades. Research and extensive studies in this field have allowed the food experts to create a diet that could provide a solution to all the health problems whether its obesity, cardiac diseases, diabetes, cholesterol, etc. For every family structure, such a diet finds a great importance. This cookbook is therefore written to provide all the secrets of the ketogenic diet. After a precise and accurate account of the ketogenic diet, the book discloses a number of tempting recipes to suit everyone's daily needs including desserts, breakfasts, exotic entrees, and homely meals.